360° degrees of Life

Things U may NOT learn in school

All rights reserved. No part of this book may be reproduced in any form without prior permission of the publisher, except for brief quotations embodied in a critical essay, article, or review. Such articles or reviews must state the correct title, author, and publisher of this book by name.

Published in the United States by
Prometheus Publishing, LLC
Please address all queries to Prometheus Publishing,
c/o 360 DoL, LLC. 719 Louise Drive, Lakeland FL 33803

Prometheus Publishing books are now available at special rates for bulk purchases, and in digital formats. Contact the publisher at the above address.

© January, 2023 by 360 DoL, LLC.
ISBN: 979-8-9879769-1-3
360 DoL, division of Prometheus Publishing, LLC
Cover design by Dorothy Amsden.

360 Degrees of Life

I dedicate this book to my son Krish Nair,
who is fond of saying:

"Bro, I know... If I don't, I'll learn it."

He often reminds me that,

Teens already know everything they need to know.

Still wondering why I started to write this book...

Acknowledgements

My Vocab is not that great and I'm thrifty, so I don't have enough words to Thank ALL the real forces that helped me with this Book. I'm gonna try anyway to mix it all in. I believe it takes a freakin' AWESOME team of open minded people to dare to be a part of a radically intellectual book idea.

First and foremost, I want to Thank my ever-patient, long-suffering wife, Vany, for not knocking me out for saying "shhhhh" to her, when I was riding some train of thought she was unaware of. Thanks to my son Krish, whenever he was around, my coffee cup was always refilled with a fresh brew. I'm forever Thankful to the teachers who taught me the ABC's and my loving parents who taught me the ABC's of Life.

I want to Thank my golfing buddy, Howard, for giving me the idea of personalizing the book using funny memes that the people can connect with. The life experiences I shared with my friends Babin M, Rahul D, Shaishiv A, Ajay Rao, Kiran Sandhu and Raju A, definitely taught me some valuable life lessons that helped me with more than one section of the book, and I Thank each of them for their contributions.

I'm eternally grateful to Rajendran P, my honorary brother figure and his compassionate better half Khushmand R, who stood by me during every struggle and all my successes. They not only mentored me but together with the Tingleys, took in an extra mouth to feed when they didn't have to.

Thanks to my mother-in-law for introducing me to my author/publisher/friend Bart Jackson and editor Lorraine Jackson who not only edits his work but patiently edits him as well. After one of our business meetings, I said, "Bart, I am writing a book," as Bart returned from being gray in shock, I continued, "and I hope your company will publish it for me." After a few weeks in recovery, Bart was ready to set on the journey with me to fulfill my dream work.

360 Degrees of Life

Thanks to the language expertise of Christian Kirkpatrick, Lorraine Jackson and Bart Jackson, my core Editorial group, my ideas are now understandable to others. Thanks to Dorothy Amsden, my marvelous graphics and layout expert, setting aside her pain and agony from surgery, put on her creative hat, and gave colors to my imagination by introducing graphics galore with support from the AI bots of Midjourney and stunning photography by Manojkumar M. Thanks to Carol Ezzo for stitching up all the material and making it sellable and shareable. Together they made my publishing dreams a reality! Not enough words to Thank...

Having an idea and turning it into a book was definitely harder than it sounded. The path that led me to the writing of this book started with my deeper involvement with Scouting and the advanced training and commitments I took on. And I Thank Mike Humphries, Tina McGuire, Rick Michels, Jason Wikman, who initiated the journey. Each of them had a piece of the puzzle to my bigger picture. To further their efforts I got help from senior staff leaders like Eric Perron, Randall MacDonald and Jennifer Combee. It sure has been a journey with reassurances from friends like Ronel Jasmine, Ryan Murphy, Scott Dutton.

Heartfelt Thanks to Nicole Hahn, for her untiring patience and mentorship throughout my vision quest for this book from the very beginning. Special Thanks to the Eldert family and especially Sianna Eldert for helping me with her graphics expertise. Thanks to Juan Alvarez for his help with graphics design and ideas. Thanks to David Faussett and Beth McCauley for their steady words of encouragement and support.

I want to Thank Everyone who ever said anything positive to me or taught me something. If I missed anyone specifically, either they have gone out of town, or they legally changed their names and didn't tell me.

Above all I Thank God.

Foreword

It's inescapable. Once you cross the threshold into those mystical, exciting "Teen Years," our culture (perhaps every culture) nails a sign to your chest announcing "I Desperately Need My Life Planned." And you quickly learn that you are a target for an advice avalanche, which you simply cannot outrun.

I remember getting mine. At any gathering with adults, I would stand politely inattentive, while every parent, relative, or counselor with the sole credentials of being "my elder" rolled out his personal wisdom and experiential tales. In retrospect, some of these well-intentioned words were wise and have proved of great value. Yet mostly what got gleaned was, "You can be anything you want, my son, and here is what you want to be…"

So it continues today. The slender reed of free will gets trampled under the heavy machinery we employ to pave the strict, narrow avenues for our teens' futures. And young adults, behaving surprisingly like real people, turn away. After several hours daily of school lectures, they don't crave more mandated directions. Instead, teens gaze wide-eyed upon the horizons of adulthood and seek to explore. They want to discover all those paths and options they know are just waiting out there. If given a free hand, they eagerly reach out to test and try the best and most fun.

And this is where *360 Degrees of Life* blows in unapologetically with a steady, strong, sorely needed breath of fresh air. Author Hary Nair has offered a lonely planet Life Guidebook for young adult explorers. He spreads before the reader a wide smorgasbord of choices to make, along with valued, clever tools to tuck into your belt. With a light heart and ready wit, Hary distills digestible ways of conducting your life.

Here, let me show the value of making new friends… Hey, have you seen what happens when you doggedly persist toward a goal that you really want, but seems such a struggle to reach?… Oh, and take a look at this man who chose to find happiness through contributing to others.

Using the succinct, get-right-to-it language of teen text-talk, the author holds out applications for your consideration – explains how each one plays out – and then lets you take it from there. Nothing preachy, these pages merely bring up what the author calls "Gentle Reminders of things U might already know."

360 Degrees of Life

And slowly it dawned on this reader: these pages are filling my forge with a selection of tools so that I may better hammer out my own character. Hary fires back to life this vital concept too often neglected in our era of outcome obsession and self-brand spinning. He gently reminds us that character – that self-essence each one of us creates – serves as our own constant companion, brought to bear on every objective we choose to pursue.

This book is a natural outpouring from its optimistic author. I first encountered Hary's plain-spoken wisdom when he brought his immense tech wizardry to help me launch first an online business journal, then Prometheus Publishing. Invariably, Hary greeted each of my wildly ambitious schemes with a knowing smile and the reply, "Anything is possible, Bart... I am here to help you fulfill your dream." Hary gave philosophic range to the term Tech Support.

Later, Hary moved on to set up a series of retail stores, with racks sporting his own T-shirt wisdoms, such as "My Life is My Style." Hary explains to customers that life joyfully created requires neither image or audience. When penning my own books, ranging from *CEO of Yourself* to *Behind Every Successful Woman is Herself*, Hary has offered up his own savvy commentary to, as promised, help me fulfill my dream.

So if you are currently blessed with teenagers or young adults in your home, leave this book out for them to browse. Then quietly, when no one is looking, pick up a copy for yourself, so you can read and select from the rich groaning board. Feast on the choices the chapters offer you. Ponder the innumerable tools and options available for navigating your tricky, confusing life.

If you are left to your own devices, I'll bet ten cents of my own money, you will make mostly the choices that benefit you. You'll see what works better, brings you greater joy, enriches your days – and you'll go for it. In other words, you'll make the right choices. And as a side bet, I'll wager a quarter that your child will too. It's just that she's a little quicker, and sees things with less-clouded eyes, so she'll arrive at the best decisions more rapidly than you. 'Tis the gift of youth.

Bart Jackson
CEO of Prometheus Publishing

Praise for 360 Degrees of Life

360 Degrees of Life is for U... Hary has narrated Life Lessons in a fun and satirical way. He shares stories from his life to talk about life and challenges and perspectives which may seem obvious but written through his lens. I encourage readers to pick this book because it has something for everyone in the pie and each slice (chapter) enlighten the reader to reflect and be motivated about seeing the *360 Degrees of Life*.

Kiran deep Sandhu
Leadership Coach, entrepreneur and educator, Malaysia

360 Degrees of Life (Things U May NOT Learn in School) meets today's youth where they are at and speaks directly to them, not at them, using their own shorthand style of writing to connect and share some of life's wisdoms in an unassuming way. Hary is not afraid to share times where he has been made a fool and how that made him feel, but more importantly what he learned from it. Since reading *360 Degrees of Life*, I have already found myself quoting some of the simple truths, like TEAM means "Together Everyone Achieves More," to my son in the car on the way to soccer practices. Being a college economics professor, I love how Hary is able to bring in some powerful economic concepts, like opportunity cost and profits, in a way that is understandable and useful. As a father involved in Scouting, I also enjoyed how Hary was able to share some of the program's goal setting advice and qualities that youth can choose to make part of their character. Each chapter ends with a prompt for notes to be made by the reader. I have no doubt that if parents and children read this together, that they would find more common ground and begin to have some relationship changing conversations. I have never read a book like this and I give it two thumbs – way up!

Dr. Patrick Ryan Murphy
Professor of Economics, Florida, US

Join author Hary Nair on a free-flowing journey of self-awareness and discovery designed to free readers from self-imposed limitations on personal and professional success. Tips and tricks, inspirational quotes, and practical guidelines are sprinkled throughout. Personal motivation, success and happiness, life choices, winning attitudes and habits; take Hary's word for it, and grow to lead a more fulfilling life!

R. MacDonald
author, educator and a volunteer with Boy Scouts of America, US

360 Degrees of Life

360 Degrees of Life
Things U May NOT learn in school

Acknowledgements i
Foreword iii
Praise for 360 Degrees of Life v
Why Shud U Read this?? ix
Introduction x

1. **I Know That** 1
2. **Believe It** 11
3. **Pro-Act, ReAct or Respond** 29
4. **Define Ur Success and Happiness** 41
5. **What's Ur Motivation??** 57
6. **Choices** 69
7. **Winning Attitudes and Habits** 87
8. **Sellable Skills 4 Ur Life** 115
9. **What U Do with What U Have ???** 129
10. **ProcrastiNation** 143
11. **Be NICE** 157
12. **Same Life – New Vibes** 169

References 177
Author's Bio 178

Why should yoU read this ??

Because U picked it up anyway.

Because U DESERVE to know Better.

Because U DO want to become Happier in Life.

Because U DO want to become Successful in Life.

Because U Believe that you have NOT learned it ALL in school.

Because U probably WILL come across something U didn't know.

Because U know that there's more to Life than what you have learned so far.

Because U will not learn some of the things talked about here from any place else.

Because U are like the REST of US wondering if you missed out any tricks to the game called Life.

Just like the Stop Sign or Yield sign you see all around the intersecting roads. The majority of things discussed in this book I'm sure U have **heard** or **talked about**. But unless U are using them, they hold no value. So I invite U to use the words in this book as a **gentle reminder** for the things U might already know.

Remember, the Stop sign on the road is an obvious one. When U approach an intersection of roadways U gotta **STOP**, **LOOK** and then **GO**. Perhaps U can Use the ideas of this book the same way.

360 Degrees of Life

Introduction

Most of the things U will read in this book come from my experiences rubbing shoulders with others, finding out what they have and what they have gone through. U R probably familiar with Facebook's clever and joyful memes. The ones used throughout the book are more familiar to my Son because the meme face is My Own. I do not claim ownership of most of the graphics used in the book. They are there merely to illustrate ideas. The graphics have been borrowed from various sources; some of the sources are not even clear, thanks to popular social media platforms and online hubs of wisdom sharing. So anything U find of value has made its way from numerous sources, including my personal life experiences and opinions.

The writing style used here is very informal and appropriate for the internet age. This is not a textbook. It is more of a guidebook for U, for the different stages of Ur life.

U are NOT to be offended by anything written here or anything in general. **Really!!**

Excuse **Urself** if U think something is offending U or if something does not align with Ur belief system. U don't have to follow everyone or everything U hear and see. After all it is Ur Life and U choose how U want to Live and what U want to believe. These ideas are just fodder for Ur own decisions.

A lot of quotations have been used throughout the book and explanations thereof. Sources have been cited as far as possible. Others are implied and there is no attempt made here to establish ownership in any way. If U claim something U find that belongs to U, please contact me and I will give the credit due to U in our next edition. A lot of famous people's names have been used for reference purposes, and if U R one of them please DO write back to me. My contact info is given in the author's bio section.

This book is an attempt to lay before U various concepts of life, **most** of which are **mostly** useful to **most** of us. I am asking U to try for Urself some of the things described in this book. They might actually help U and change Ur perspective on things for the better.

The style adopted here is that of a casual CHAT vs. a written lecture. I hope U enjoy it and find Wisdom at Ur leisure.

I Know That...

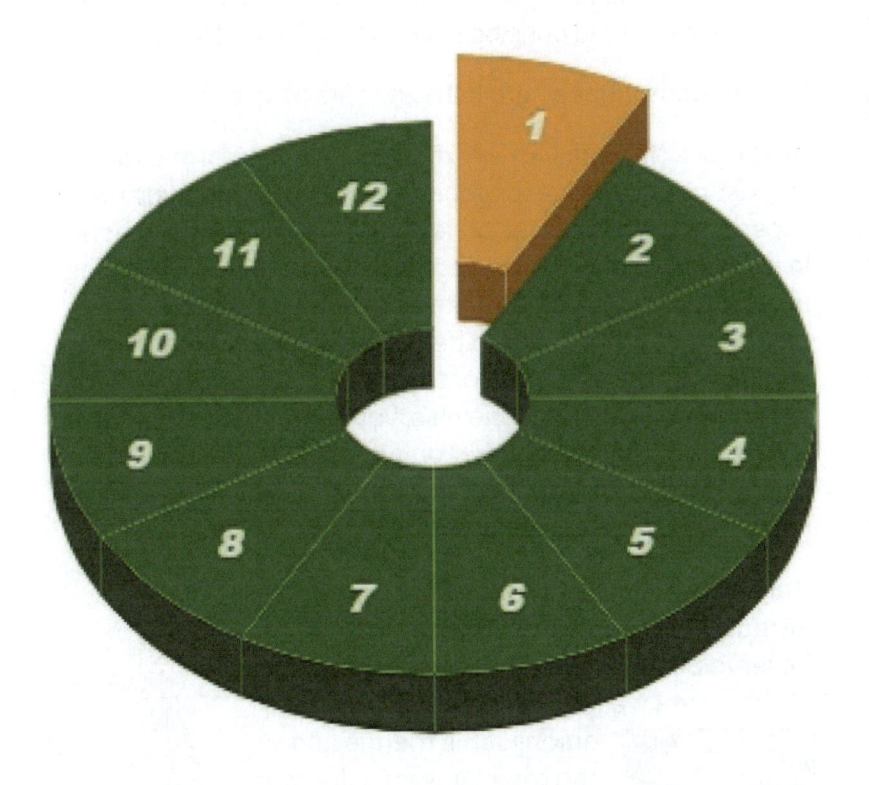

I Know That ...

The 3 most dangerous words in English.

"I know that..." is one of the most dangerous combinations of words in the English language when it comes to personal progress. The productive years of our life are usually the journey from the teen years when our slogan is "I Know That..." to the phase where our slogan becomes "I wish I knew that... ."

Life happens somewhere in the middle of all that.

As U move through life, Ur experiences add information into Ur existing knowledge for good or for worse, depending on Ur experiences and sources of new information. Ur first teachers in life will probably be the people around while U R growing up – Ur parents, siblings, relatives or school teachers. Ur last teacher for sure is going to be Ur Experiences. Whether it is something you are trying for the first time or you watched and learned from someone else, your **personal experience** will be your very last teacher on any topic in life. The old saying holds true – Ur experiences will give U either a nice memory to Treasure or a valuable lesson to Remember.

During my teen years ATMs were being introduced in India and I was visiting the Reserve Bank where my father worked at the time. I walked in on a conversation amongst his friends and the topic of discussion was the introduction of ATMs into the various banks in the city. This was the pre-internet era and very few people had any idea about these new machines. I heard one of his friends asking another one in the group, "so, what is an ATM?" and of course I was the teen there, and of course 'I knew it', and of course I had to outsmart the adults. So I jumped in on

360 Degrees of Life

the conversation and said, "Oh, it is the Any Time Money machine." There was total silence, they looked over to me, gave a 5 second pause before they all **LoL-ed** at me. I heard a familiar voice come as a saving grace; my Dad spoke up and said, "It's actually Automated Teller Machines, son, where you can get Money out Any Time you want, whether the bank is open or closed." That was the first day I remember that I made a fool of myself, because at the time I believed "I know that...". Remember Ur Own "I know that..." moments??

Ever since that incident I became cautious when I said, "I know that...". I had learned my lesson that half knowledge is more risky than we can think of. Not only do we make a fool out of ourselves but sometimes having half the knowledge and passing it on creates a bigger risk to those around U. This happens if U R in a position of Authority and Ur team relies on Ur knowledge. Leadership demands that U have to be more careful and more responsible before U jump in to say "I know that..." Now that I look back, "I wish I had..." heard of this quote from *Abraham Lincoln*, "Better to remain silent and be thought a fool than to speak and to remove all doubt."

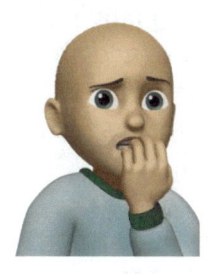

When it comes to life choices, principles and strategies, it is very easy to say, "I know that", "I've Heard about that", "I've Read about that", etc. In reality none of that means a thing, what really matters is R U using any of that knowledge Now?? If you are, then R U using it in a Systematic way to produce the best desired results? Most often than not, we don't use knowledge properly or in a systematic way, because mostly we lack one of the most desirable qualities, **patience**.

I know that...

7 centuries ago, an English poet, William Langland spoke wisely that "Patience is a virtue." How True. Patience is the accepted reality that we are **not** always in control. Patience is a complex quality that covers self-control and tolerance too. To do anything systematically, you **definitely** need patience and organizational skills, both of which can be learned and developed over time. People often get all worked up over situations where they have no control anyway. They may feel they know everything about the situation, yet they actually have no control on it. Classic example wud be a traffic jam. In Ur viewpoint, **U know** where U R going, **U know** how long it shud take, **U know** U planned for the normal conditions and added a few extra minutes in the planning for the unexpected. But who wud have thought to add an extra 2 hours into the trip planning for the 7 car pile up in front of U? Life has just spun totally out of control despite all the planning and all the things U Knew about the trip. Welcome to the Real World!! This is a situation where Ur Patience comes into play. There is no point getting upset about the situation, there is nothing U can do but to wait through the scenario to move ahead. In short, there are situations in life when U might Know Everything U need to Know about a situation, and still it could be out of Ur total control. So teach Urself **not to worry but to Live through it**. The situations always change.

Sometimes, things are not as simple as they appear. What may appear to be one of the "I know that..." situations becomes a bit more complex when U look at the details. Let us go and grab a bag of simple Regular potato chips.

> **INGREDIENTS:** POTATOES, VEGETABLE OIL (CANOLA, CORN, SOYBEAN, AND/OR SUNFLOWER OIL), AND SALT.

If you look at the ingredients as shown, it is very simple.

We might all say, "I know that..." it's just Potatoes, Oil and Salt. We also know how the end result should look and that the end result should taste a little crisp, a little salty and easy to

360 Degrees of Life

consume. We have a mental picture of how it should all work out as well, something like this:

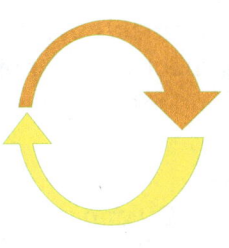

So the real question is how to get from the picture on the left to the picture on the right. To do that we will need some degree of patience and some detailed instructions as well. Yes, we all know potatoes, oil and salt. But how to use them properly to produce the desired result determines if we are getting good chips to enjoy or something to talk about as a bad experiment. This is a typical scenario where instructions or coaching also comes to play. **Coaching** – the tool U need when U think U know that… but U really don't.

Just like the potato chips, in Ur life, U will be dealing with new situations, most of which at the first glance will look like one of Ur "I know it…" moments. But with a little more thought U might realize that a simple guide to handle that situation might be useful. Ur best bet often is to ask someone who has been in that situation before, and done what you are trying to do. Seriously, It is **OK to Ask**. Who knows; maybe they will give you an easier way to handle the challenge. Better yet, they may tell you about Blunders to Avoid . My father used to often remind me that a wise person is the one who can learn from other people's experiences, especially the mistakes. Wise person always learns from Success and Failures – Ur own and those of Others.

Now U might say, "I knew that…, and I do ask others for help," but there is a slight difference between asking for help and asking for guidance. Asking for help can be as simple as saying, "Can you please come help me move this table?" Asking for Guidance can be trickier. Some of U may feel that seeking guidance shows weaknesses. May hate to admit out loud that "I don't know it" because this chips away at Ur pride or casts doubts on Ur abilities. But it doesn't have to be like that, it is all in the perspective. Most of the time with a little help from others the end result can be more **rewarding** and **satisfying**.

Actually, asking for both Guidance and Quality help is a sign of good leadership skills. U R using all the resources at Ur command to effectively achieve Ur goals. By asking another person for help, U are stepping out of Ur comfort zone. That is often the first and most critical step you can take towards **personal improvement** – stepping out of your comfort zone. In a recent *New York Times* interview, the Barstool Sports CEO said, "Any young person should, at some point, take a job that makes them uncomfortable and that they feel unqualified for. It's really great to feel uncomfortable, and you change so much as a person from that."[1] High achievers are normally the first ones stepping out of their comfort zones, U can be one of them too. Success and Happiness, as they say, are usually just outside the boundaries of Ur personal comfort zone. Here's a funny saying for the situation,

At age 20
We **worry** about what Others think of us.
At age 40,
We **don't care** what Others think of us.
At age 60,
we **discover** they **Haven't been thinking** of us at all.

OMG

It shud not be that hard to step out of Ur comfort zone, because seriously nobody is watching, and nobody cares as much as U think. To get ahead in life in general, U need to sometimes whittle away a little bit of that stubborn portion of ego that believes that U can do anything by Urself and U don't need anyone else to live in this world – because **U know it all**. Just by taking some help U R not giving away anything. U don't have to prove anything to anyone, not even to Urself. Whatever U do in life, it shud not be to prove anything to anybody, because that will not bring U any joy, once the proving part is over.

The Great Work Study, conducted by the O.C. Tanner Institute, showed that 72% of people who receive awards for their work ask for advice, help, insights, and opinions from people outside of their inner circle.[1] Asking for help from others also builds a strong bond with them as U are demonstrating to them that U value their opinions and U trust their skill sets, to do the job at hand. In essence U actually build a team of trustworthy people around U by simply asking for help and letting go of that ego state of "I know that..." and "I can do that by myself." There is a beautiful acronym for **TEAM** that says Together Everyone Achieves More and how true that is. This is why no matter how much U believe that U know it all, it will always be more fulfilling to achieve Ur Goals as a Team.

Lot of times, people will leave their team or company simply because they feel undervalued. **If U do not feel valued**, don't get angry at the situation. U R just in the wrong place. This does NOT undermine Ur abilities or Ur skill set. Move on to a different place, a different team or different company – be the right person at the right place at the right time. Those who know Ur value will always appreciate U for who U R and what U bring to the team. Just because U know a lot more than Ur team will not make U valuable to the team, unless U use Ur knowledge and skills for the betterment of the team as a whole. You may be a legendary person, but to those around U the only thing that matters is how Ur presence is making a positive influence on them.

I know that...

U can be looking at something and think that U know everything about it – U may be 100% right in one scenario while U may be wrong from a totally different perspective. Look at the simple illustration below from a social media source called @successpictures. It is so simple yet so profound. Shown here is a scenario where 4 different individuals view the exact same thing in 4 completely different ways. Everyone is looking at the same simple Tree.

To the 1st person the Tree is just a source of raw material for his construction business, while for the logger, it is just a tree trunk. For the carpenter it is material for building his furniture, while for the kid it's just a Tree. Are they looking at the same thing? Yes, but are they viewing it completely differently? Is any of them wrong in their viewpoint?? NO. Is any of them wrong in general?? NO. If U live under the perception that only Ur viewpoint is correct because **U Know It**, Count on It – U will face obstacles all along the way in life. So, Yes, DO see things from Ur own perspective but be Wise and Understand the other person's perspective also. This topic is further discussed in Chapter 6: Choices.

360 Degrees of Life

Now I know that...

I know that...

360 Degrees of Life

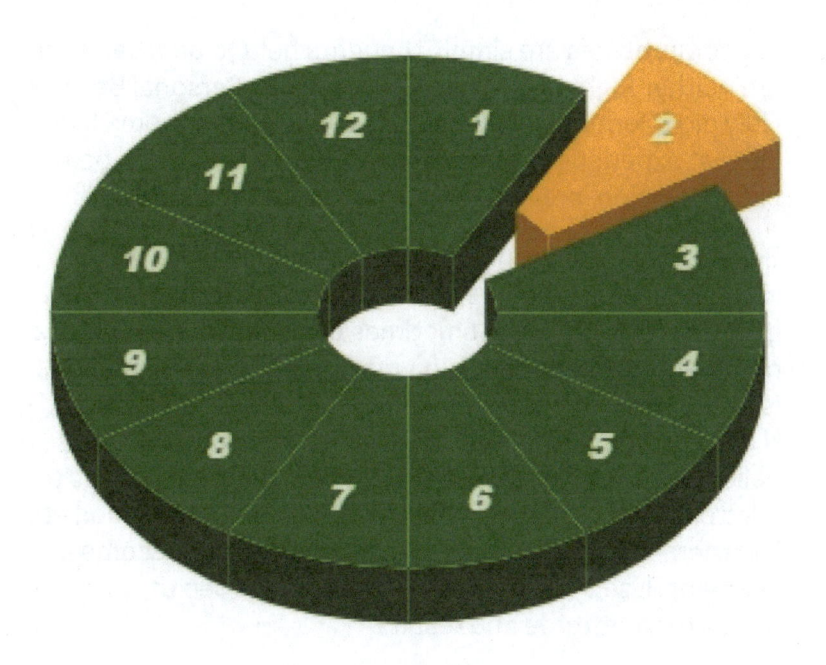

Believe It...

Believe It...

11

Believe it...

U didn't bring Anything into this world, but U have a Lot to Learn from it.

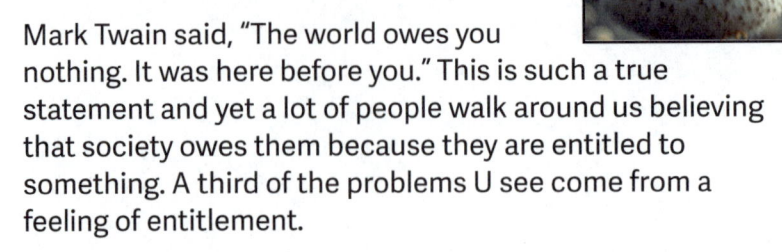

Mark Twain said, "The world owes you nothing. It was here before you." This is such a true statement and yet a lot of people walk around us believing that society owes them because they are entitled to something. A third of the problems U see come from a feeling of entitlement.

For some, beliefs are simply thoughts held to be true – they are neither Right nor Wrong. So, what R Ur Personal Beliefs? How did U form them? R they just strong opinions drawn from Ur past experiences or the hearsay of others?? Such beliefs color Ur vision, preventing U from seeing the world as it is.

Beliefs are usually conclusions V draw up when V are young with much less exposure to the world and much less experience in general. Sometimes our belief system plays a dominant role in our decision making abilities too, and this is how Ur true beliefs become Ur self-fulfilling prophecies. U act according to Ur beliefs, and Ur actions follow those beliefs to make them a reality. Believe in the power of positive 4-letter words like Love, Hope, Best, Fair, Real, Help, Good etc. Put them in the right perspective and they can become life changing. Use them to guide Ur actions and see the magic it brings to Ur attitude and results.

If U were to interview the average person on the street, they wud probably tell U how horrible our society is becoming, how things are *transforming* from bad to worse in most avenues of life. The families are redefining themselves, relationships are redefining themselves, divorce rates are going up, the rate of violence is going up, there R school shootings, mass shootings, hate crimes and everything else U can imagine. U might wonder how U can survive in such a negative world; U might even think that the hope for a better future is almost fading away.

360 Degrees of Life

I know it... ***Life is Not Easy at Ur age***.
How do **V** survive in a world like this??

🔑 **Accept Responsibility** – U need to **accept responsibility** for Ur actions, Ur performance and Ur conduct. Whatever U do, make sure they are always legal, moral and ethical, because there is overwhelming proof which shows that the good guys and the good gals, who have good ethics and act with integrity, really R the ones who end up with all the good things life has to offer. That includes most of the things that money will buy and ALL of the things that money cannot buy. So what happens down the road of life should be of concern to U. 99% of the time U can predict Ur future based on Ur actions. If the intentions are strong enough and U R willing to work towards it, results are almost guaranteed. Always plan for contingencies along the way.

🔑 **Cash Benefits** – Most of U must have heard the common cliches like, **money** will buy you a good bed, but it cannot buy you a good night's rest. Money will get you plenty of **fair-weather friends**, the ones who are around when U R in a sunny spot in life, but only a **good character base** will get U a **true friend**, one who will stand by U – through thick and thin. Money and wealth can bring U a bunch of materialistic stuff, but most of those things U can live without, and most of those things U cannot take with U when U leave this world either.

🔑 **Be the Change** – If U don't like what U R living through, **become the change**. "Be the change U want to see in the world", a simple yet powerful statement made by Mahatma Gandhi. U say politics is dirty and U stay out of it. Well guess what happens and who gets in it? If U need to change it, get involved in Ur community, Ur politics. Let the good guys and the good gals take charge and make the much needed change. If U think the situation shud change, be the Change and make it happen.

Believe It...

🗝️ **Don't Compare** – Please Don't compare Urself to anyone. There is Not another one of U in this whole wide world. U R as **Unique** and as good as it gets. Where U start Ur life is not an important thing, but where U GO from there – that is the significant thing. U have a responsibility to Urself to give Ur best at everything U do. Always keep in mind that there is an opportunity cost involved in every decision you make. If U want to be the best, U gotta pay the price for it, whether it is in terms of time or effort.

🗝️ **Size of Ur dream** – It is rightly said that it's NOT the **color** of Ur skin or the place of Ur **birth** that determines Ur future; it is the size of the dream that U carry in Ur heart and the **determination** that U have to achieve those dreams and goals that makes a world of difference. John H. Johnson, Founder of Johnson Publishing Company and *Ebony* magazine and the first African American to appear on Forbes 400 said, "Men and women are not limited by the place of their birth, not by color of their skin, but by the size of their hope." It is the size of Ur hope that determines where U finally end up in Ur life. Walt Disney said, "If you can Dream it; You can Do it". Dreams have no expiration date, and as long as U have dreams of doing something or achieving something, there is always hope for a future.

🗝️ **Do Ur Best** – Whatever U do, DO it as if this is the **Last job** U R going to do for Ur career, and this is the final unit of measurement to determine Ur success. Basically give it Ur Best. Now, apply this attitude to every aspect of Ur life and see what a change that will be..

🗝️ **Conquer Failure** – U have probably heard that, U will fail at some point in Ur life. It may not be in school or college or even personal life, but U will fail at some point. Accept it. U will lose and probably embarrass Urself too. U cannot be master of everything. Like they say, Every master was once a disaster. I'm sure the 1st time Beethoven was on that piano, he did NOT impress his neighbors or relatives. Everyone gets knocked down at some point in life; Ur true success is then determined by **how fast U get back up** and back on track moving towards Ur goals. The one who falls and gets back up to move ahead, is SO much better than the one who never tried at all.

In 1776 there were roughly less than **3 million Americans** alive, and those 3 million Americans produced people like George Washington, Benjamin Franklin, Alexander Hamilton, Thomas Jefferson, and the list goes on. At the time of the writing of this book, **Americans** are **330+ million** strong, and they have produced ...
I challenge U to come up with the names of 1 or 2 people who have the character, the commitment, the accomplishments, the intellect that these founding leaders of America had.
U need people like that today more than ever before, people who have **values**, **beliefs**, those who make **commitments**, those who **accept responsibility**, those who have an interest in **OTHER people's** welfare, people whose **word** IS their Bond. **TRUST** is that Crazy glue that holds our society together. What is happening to that Trust factor, where is the Love among Us humans?? What happened, what went wrong, where did we miss it ???????

Why it is so, what happened along the way in the last 200+ years that changed it all?? According to the Thomas Jefferson Research Institute, back then over 90% of education focussed on building **character** and supporting **religious faith**. By 1926, the percentage had dropped down to just 6%,

Believe It...

15

Believe It...

and by the 1950s the percentage of character and faith included in the educational process was so LOW that it was almost impossible to measure. So the question V need to ask ourselves is, Does character count?? Does faith count?? Does having the right concept of what life is all about count?? These shud be questions that keep U awake at night, because the answers to these might pave the way for a better future V all talk about... think about it, and Believe in the possibilities.

U might ask, "Well **what do I do** to fix all this messy ...?"
To begin with, STOP depending on the society to support Ur lifestyle, like someone owes U something. The world doesn't owe U anything. Are U surprised??!! Well the world that U see now was here long before U came along... so how does the world owe U?? Get that idea of entitlement OUT of Ur mind and get real. **Start** taking care of Urself and Ur personal needs. Then take care of Ur family needs. Then reach over and start helping those others who R not as capable or are less fortunate than U. So, take that first step, **Start believing in Urself**. U know U can Do it. Take care of Urself.

Character is defined by the set of Qualities that marks U as Distinctive and Honorable. Now when U remove the importance of character from the education system, U R already on a downhill slope, a slope so slippery that it is almost impossible to climb back up. George Bernard Shaw wisely said, "**Progress** is impossible without change, and those who cannot change their minds cannot change anything." So, **Believe in Urself** and believe that U can become the change that U **so** want to see in Ur society. There is nothing stopping U except Ur own **self-limiting beliefs**. Such negative perceptions are the most dangerous of all things in Ur mind. If U think a change this big is too much for U, kiss Ur Dreams GoodBye. Instead, if U take ownership of Every action U take

360 Degrees of Life

and make sure U impact the people around U in a positive way, Ur actions will have a far-reaching effect. When more people start believing in themselves and act like this, **a Wave of Change** is created, and the rest will be history. Remember every Revolution starts with a single person. Henry Ford was fond of saying that whether you think you can or you think lyou can't, **YOU are RIGHT**. When U think U can handle a task, then Ur brain is already figuring out ways to do it. That is just the way our minds work.

U don't have to be great to start making differences in other people's lives, but U gotta start making differences in Ur own life. Unless U start making changes, U cannot see progress. And if U R not growing U R withering. Just like a plant. If it's not growing, it's definitely dying; slowly but surely. So U decide.

Break Free of Ur Trained Limitations

Just like the horse tied to the empty chair does not move because it was trained as a pony that when there is a rope around its neck its movement is restricted to the length of the rope, most of the time U are restricted by the people around U who constantly pass on their fears and failures onto Ur mind. It gets so bad that by the time U reach adolescence there is a huge build up of self-limiting beliefs in Ur mind. It takes a lot of courage to break that chain of self-limiting belief and come out of the shell, but once U step outside, there is a whole new world waiting for you to explore. The only way to achieve this seemingly impossible task is by actually starting to believe that it is **Possible**.

The Fire of Imagination

Anytime U approach a task using Ur knowledge alone, U R limiting Urself, instead if U approach with a broader imagination, U open a whole new world of possibilities. Maybe that is why **Einstein** said something like the true sign of **intelligence** is not how much knowledge U have, but how much **imagination** U have. Knowledge is often limited, but imagination knows no bounds.

Here's a story about the power of **imagination**. It was a Monday after winter break at school, and the regular teacher was absent so we had a substitute teacher who asked us to give a short tale about an exciting event from our winter break. Everyone had stories to share, and then came little Tommy's turn. He came to the front of the class and started the story of how he went to the mountains for camping with his father and went ice fishing in the lake and so forth. Then, one morning as they were returning from the lake, they were faced with a family of great big grizzly bears, all 3 of them. The papa bear weighed, oh, about 700 some pounds while the mama bear looked about 500 some pounds. Surprisingly the 200-some-pound baby bear started running towards the father and they went out of sight chasing each other, while little Tommy was left alone to fight the 2 big bears. All he had in his defense was a pistol his father had dropped while running away from the baby bear. He went on explaining how he bravely tackled the 2 big bears one at a time and pinned them to the ground before his father returned to the scene. His father was so proud that he promised to buy him a gift of his choice after they returned home from the mountains. At this point the teacher was exhausted from the fable, asked Tommy to go back to his seat, and commented that it was definitely a cock and bull story.

Tommy asked the teacher why she thought it was a fable. The teacher responded, "If I told the class that this morning on my way to school, I saw a little fox terrier being attacked by 2 rottweilers, and the fox terrier jumped up a lamp post and landed on one of the rottweilers, breaking its neck, while it scratched the eyeballs out of the other one before it ran back home to its owners." The teacher asked, "Would anyone in class believe my story?" And little Tommy jumped up and said, "Oh yes ma'm, I will believe it. As a matter of fact, that was **MY** white fox terrier that you saw, and I call him **Snowy**."

There is really no bounds to imagination, so the only thing that stops U is Ur beliefs. Start Believing in Urself. Use Ur imagination, be somewhat realistic and create a **Vision** for Ur future. **Believe** in Urself and believe that U can achieve it. Have action plans to achieve those goals within Ur vision and most importantly **Follow Through**.

Many of U who are reading this would agree that **Ur self-limiting beliefs become Ur self-fulfilling prophecies**. For example, if U believe that U are not as qualified for a high-paying job in Ur industry then U will apply for a lower paying job and U will land up in the low-paying job just **as U believed**. If U believe U R not smart enough for a higher education, U will stop making efforts unknowingly to attain a higher education and hence never attain that higher education **as U believed**. If U believe U R not smart enough to be a business owner, then U will not try to start Ur own business and thus U will never be a business owner **as U believed**. If U believe that real estate is not Ur cup of tea and U cannot make money in real estate, U will never try to invest in real estate and hence U will never make money from it, just **as U believed**. It has been proven time and again by various people that if U believe in something wholeheartedly and work towards it there is pretty much nothing to stop U except Ur own belief. If U choose a realistic goal, U can always reach it.

Believe It...

People of Value

The famous cartoonist Charles Schulz once said: The people who make a difference in Ur life are NOT the ones with the most credentials, the most money or the most awards. If U don't believe it ... read through the following set of questions for Urself:

1. Name the top 3 wealthiest people in the world today.
2. Name the last 3 Nobel prize winners.
3. Name the last 3 Academy Award winners.
4. Name the 3 most valuable inventors of this century.

Could U answer all of them? None of the above names actually matter beyond a point, they keep changing, not because they are second-rate achievers but because the applause always eventually dies, awards tarnish over time, achievements are forgotten and accolades and certificates are often buried with their owners. Now read through the following questions and see how well U fare:

1. Name 3 teachers who helped U in Ur journey through school.
2. Name 3 friends who helped U through a difficult time.
3. Name 3 people who have taught U something worthwhile.
4. Name 3 people who have made a difference in Ur life.
5 Name 3 people U enjoy spending time with.

Now this second set of questions was easier to deal with, right?? Y was that?? Because those questions were about rich and famous people or because they were people who actually meant something to U personally?? U don't need to answer... V all know the Y.

360 Degrees of Life

Ur Value and What U Value

Contrary to popular belief, **everybody does NOT hate everybody else who doesn't look like themselves**[7]. If U actually work with people of different socioeconomic classes and different educational or ethnic backgrounds, U will find that they do not hate or dislike people different from themselves, unlike the stereotype where everybody thinks that everybody else hates their type.

And if U think one step further, there is plenty evidence that proves that we REALLY have some seriously common ancestry. So go ahead and Be Nice to the other person, after all they R related to U in some way. Ur belief is what alters Ur actions when U interact with others – have the right beliefs and U will be fine.

Believe it, EVERYTHING in this world becomes very important at two points in its existence – **first**, before you own it, and **second**, after you lose it. This applies to all aspects of Ur life, whether U apply it to a pricey material possession or a valuable relationship. Before U own a desirable thing – be it a higher social position, an expensive possession, a dream job, a new relationship with that person U like, a new car or anything at all – U will place immense value on that thing. However, once that object of desire has been achieved, often we start taking it for granted, it seems to lose its value or significance. This is a dangerous situation. When U forget its importance U lose interest in it, and slowly but surely U stop paying attention to it. Then like a nice flowering plant that U nurtured, it will start to wither and die. So **learn** to give importance to the things U truly desire and attach lifelong values to them. Understand that material things, things of this world, are just as easily replaceable as anything else out there. The things that truly hold value are Ur **relationships**, Ur **time** and the **memories** U build with Ur time, they are almost irreplaceable.

Believe It...

If U R not sure of this, look back to a time when U really had FUN with some Loved One in Ur life. It could be Ur Child, Ur Parent, Ur Sibling, Ur Relatives, Ur Pets, Ur Toys or Ur Friends. We always try to capture Good times or Good Memories into a Picture, Why?? Because simply looking at a picture can bring back memories of a LOT of good times U had. It is in human nature to do things for self or others that make us **feel good**. When we do things with **others** we feel more pleasure than we would if we did them by ourselves. There are only a handful of things V do as humans that V truly enjoy doing alone – do a self-check !!

There are several ways V can measure ourselves. Just **don't use someone else's metrics to measure Urself** – if at all possible. In most social scenarios humans R very quick to judge, it's second nature to most – Sad but True. Which is Y we have saying such as, "Looks can be deceiving" or "Don't judge a book by its cover." Being patient and humble when U R massively powerful or being generous and giving even when U have very little are always respectable and likable qualities. These are acts that create good vibes for U and for others. So keep the vibes flowing.

Ur whole Life can be treated as a School, because there is NO better place to Learn about Life other than Life itself. **The role of School** in Ur life is to help U get more out of Ur Experiences, because Ur Experiences are what is going to teach U the most in Life. It can be Ur own Experiences or things U learn from other peoples' experiences. Schools will teach U how to use the Tools U need for Life – how to Handle and Apply the Knowledge U have gained. Ultimately U have to decide what U want to get out of Ur school and Ur education. U have to decide what U want, then where and how to use that tool of Knowledge.

360 Degrees of Life

Just like a small key is all it takes to open a big lock and a small door can lead U into a large Mansion, a small Act of **Kindness** can open the doors to a lifelong relationship. A small spark of **Imagination** is all it takes to open doors to a life-altering invention. Remember, the key is never as big as the lock itself, the lock that is guarding that mansion or that room that is full of choices and opportunities. The keys U carry is what is going to determine the opportunities U open for Urself. The more open minded U R, the more opportunities and choices open up for U. The amount of knowledge U gain from Ur basic schooling is like that small key. Usually about 10-15% of Ur life lessons are learned while U R in school but that 10-15% forms the foundation for everything U can imagine to build upon for the rest of Ur lives.

Measuring Urself

Believe it, it is not that hard to measure Urself. Try using the following 4-ways :

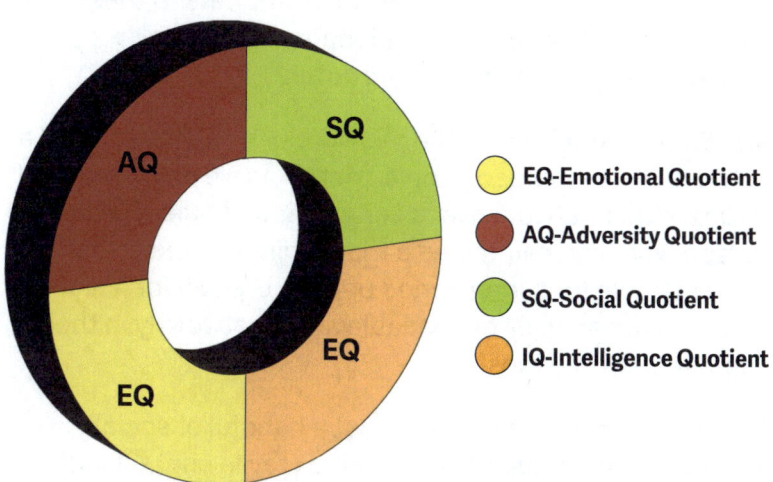

- EQ-Emotional Quotient
- AQ-Adversity Quotient
- SQ-Social Quotient
- IQ-Intelligence Quotient

Most of U are familiar with **IQ – Intelligence Quotient** – which measures Ur level of understanding, Ur ability to know and Ur brain's capacity to perceive things as they are. For example, Ur IQ levels will determine Ur ability to solve math problems or memorize concepts and recall and relate things U have learned in the past. In my opinion, IQ levels are overrated and given far more weightage in academic fields. A high IQ is definitely a very desirable trait, but it is not by any means the be-all and end-all in measuring a person.

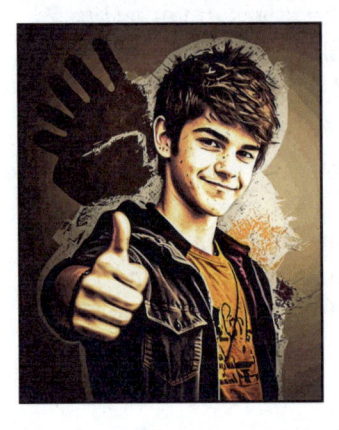

EQ - Emotional Quotient – is the measure of Ur ability to maintain peace with others. It is a measure of how U behave in interactions with others – all sorts of interactions. It measures how well U can appreciate other people's time, Ur responsibility towards others, Ur honesty in interactions, how well U can respect other people's boundaries. R U humble when dealing with others?? R U genuine with others – with people who are not even directly related to U?? R U considerate and thoughtful with others?? These are some quick factors that can help U measure Ur EQ levels. The answers to these metrics should be very self-explanatory. In short, Ur *EQ* generally represents Ur **Character**.

SQ - Social Quotient – is the measure of Ur ability to build a network of like-minded people, friends as we call them, and maintain that network over a Long Period of time. If U know a person who has maintained a friendship with more than one or two people for a long period of time, U know for a fact that they are socially dependable and trustworthy in their demeanor for the most part.

They must possess more than just a handful of socially acceptable good qualities. U tend to stay in contact with people who are loyal, dependable, trustworthy and can be open and available to U as needed. Ur **SQ** is representative of Ur **Charisma** too – Ur actual ability to attract and maintain a connection with other individuals.

People who demonstrate Good Character and are generally Friendly and Charismatic tend to go much further in life than someone who has a phenomenal IQ but lower Emotional and Social connections. Most education systems develop and hone skills to improve the IQ levels of their students, but a person of high IQ can end up being employed by a person of higher EQ and SQ who has only an average IQ.

One of the measures which most education systems do not give much importance to is the **AQ – Adversity Quotient**. This is the true measure of Ur ability to handle the adversities presented to U in life, the rough patches of life so to speak. Everyone goes through them. It is never rainbows and butterflies all the while. How U handle Urself through these tough times is what determines Ur AQ. The quickest way out is to give up – when the going gets tough the losers give up, and the ones who fight through it get to **succeed in life**. No one has achieved anything of any significance by giving up. So **don't even think about giving up**. Fight for what U believe U can achieve and don't stop until U gain it. If you don't believe in Urself, no one will believe in you. First U have to learn to believe in Urself and Ur abilities. That will make a whole world of difference.

Character : Ur Beliefs vs. Their Opinions

Be Trustworthy – trust is like a piece of paper. If U want to believe it for Urself, here is a simple experiment for U to do. Grab a piece of fresh unused paper, clean and crisp as can be. U should not have a crease or a fold in it. Now assume that this represents Ur Character – Clean and Crisp, nothing hidden, nothing tucked under the skin etc. Now crumble it, crumble it lightly or heavily, crumble it as U please. Now open it back up and hold it up to any source of light. What is Ur first observation – well, it is not Clean or Crisp, right??

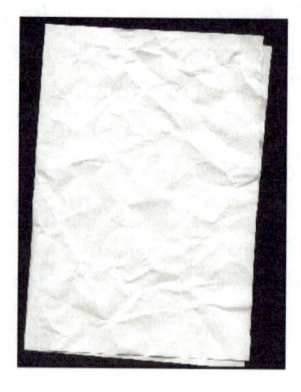

Now Do Your BEST to straighten out that SAME piece of paper and see if U can bring it back to the original Clean and Crisp form. No matter what U do, (unless U recycle it or something) U cannot make it Clean and Crisp as it was before. Ur **Character is just like that**. Once U crumble it, there is NO way to make it back to the Original form. So Watch What U Choose to Do. Always remember that crumpled paper and never let that happen to Ur Character. Coz there is no way to fix it. A patchwork always shows up as a patchwork, no matter how much U try to hide it.

Believe it... most people do believe that Heaven has everything U can desire and doesn't have **Pain**. In fact, this world of Ours has everything we need, but People don't have **Peace of Mind**. People may have everything they need to live, but they don't have **Patience**. Just as heaven is a Concept or State of Mind, so is Pain, Patience, and Peace of Mind. When U say U don't have everything U need to Live, Pause and take a closer look. Maybe this is just a thought, maybe Ur environment is forcing U to believe that U don't have everything U need. Maybe it is all about Ur State of Mind and Ur perspective on Ur situation.

Believe it... A **Fact** is just information minus the emotions people attach to it. If U hear that Ur pet just died of an illness, U are bound to get sad, because now U have attached Ur emotion to the Fact of the pet's death. An **Opinion** is usually formed when there is information present, and the information is handled by a person who has some **Experience** handling that kind of information. **Ignorance** is demonstrated when an Opinion is formed by someone lacking Experience and the person has not much Information either – a good reason to stay away from the Ignorant.

It is not necessary that everyone values U or Ur opinions the same. Most of the **scales** around are simple and can only **weigh** the quantity and cannot measure the **Quality.** So when U evaluate a thing or a person or a situation, make sure to use the correct scales to do the evaluation. Not everyone around U can like U because everyone has different tastes, the same way a few people's opinions will not make one person better than the other. Some opinions are far from Facts. Likes and Dislikes can also depend on **popularity** and social influence. While they may be options to consider, they may be totally ***irrelevant*** too.

Keep thoughts in Ur brain that will fill Ur day with Positivity and Hope. Every Day U wake Up is a Gift from Life, so treat it that way. If U don't believe that Every Single Day is a Gift to be treasured, Try missing 1 day of Ur Life... .

Believe It...

Now I believe that...

ProAct, ReAct or Respond

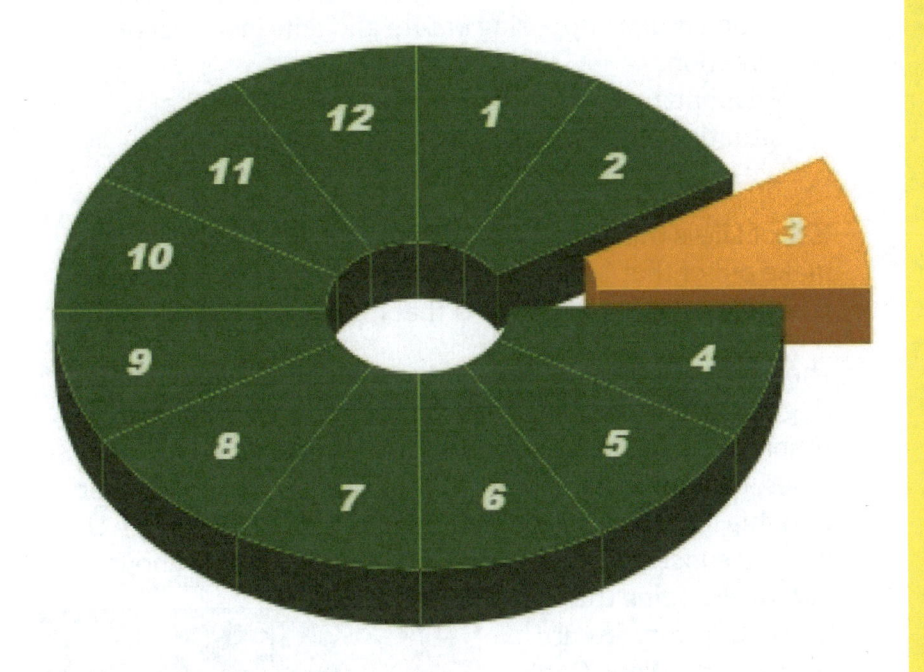

How U act will determine what U get out of Ur life

For any given situation, understand that there are ONLY 3 ways U can act. U can either ProAct, ReAct or Respond. For those who "Know it" and those who think they may not know it, let us understand the differences:

★ ProActing in a situation means to take action in advance of an expected event.
★ ReActing in a situation means to act in response to an external influence on an event or a person. Usually, the action is of an opposing nature and acts in a reverse direction.
★ Responding to a situation means to ReAct to the situation in a favorable way, as in continuing the action on the expected event.

10% of Life is things that HAPPEN to us and 90% of what we make out of that 10%. It is NOT what happens to U but how U handle what happened to U that makes a difference in life.

The way you ProAct or Respond to a situation demonstrates Ur general mental strength. To increase Ur mental strength, U simply need to change Ur outlook. When U R faced with hard times, just understand that life's challenging moments offer valuable lessons. These tough lessons build the strength U need to succeed. Developing mental strength is all about **habitually** doing the things that very few are willing to do. Wade Cook, the self proclaimed financial guru had mentioned something very insightful, that can be summarized as: if U R willing to do what most people won't do for the next few years, then U will be able to do what most people can't do, for the rest of Ur life. **Willingness** to put in the **extra effort** when it is needed is what makes all the difference in the world.

Here are a few ways that mentally strong people Proact or Respond:

★ **Fight for what U really desire** – Doing this when U feel almost defeated is a habit U can develop. When U force Urself to work through a challenge, Ur **inner strength** and confidence begins to grow. Any big challenge can be broken down into baby steps. As U take each step, U will feel more accomplished and more confident to take the next steps.

★ **Save the Best for Last** – A number of studies show the effects of saving the best for last. U don't have to eat the dessert first. **Learn to Delay gratification** and focus on the bigger visions that can only materialize when U work patiently towards them by putting in the necessary time and effort. People fall for instant gratification when they have No Hope for the Future, which is why Having Goals and Dreams or Ambitions is SO important in life.

★ **Make Mistakes** – When U are focused on achieving Ur goals and dreams, there is absolutely NO room for what other people might think about Ur failures. No human has learned to walk and run before falling down a few times then getting back up and trying harder. Don't waste Ur Time or Energy worrying about Ur failures. Sometimes, failures are nothing but a small and necessary step along Ur

Journey to Success in Life. So don't worry about mistakes. **Make mistakes**, let the people laugh at U, it is **OK**. In Ur next attempt **try Harder and Smarter**. Put Ur Energy and Focus into the Lesson U Learn FROM those failures. That will get U closer to Ur Goals more efficiently.

★ **Channel Ur Emotions** – A Bad mood shud NOT make U lash out just as a Good mood shud NOT make U callous and Overconfident. Emotions R a powerful Engine that can drive U forward but make sure Ur Brain is engaged in the Steering. Every minute spent worrying about a task is eating away the time U cud be spending on the task itself. Get in the **habit of making tough calls** – that is a learnable skill. Worrying has never Gotten anyone anywhere useful. So Y Worry much ??

★ **Trust Ur gut** – Is this fancy overrated concept?? There is a very fine line between trusting Ur gut and being impulsive. How can U decide whether U shud trust Ur gut?? Trust Ur gut when making decisions where the choices are not making logical sense but R based on Ur knowledge and expertise. Respond to Ur own calling in such cases, for example, Ur decision to say No to drugs when Ur Best Bud offers U a bud. What we call intuitions or gut calling are often our brains' way of showing us safe choices or solutions based on our past experiences and preconditioned mindset. V shud pay attention to them.

★ **Lead even when no one else follows** – If Ur vision is clear and U R willing to walk-the-walk, then lead the path by all means, even when no one else is following U. Lot of times, U will be so far ahead on the path that those following U may not have seen or understood Ur complete vision. Y not Pro-Act based on Ur knowledge and Ur vision?? Eventually others who want to support U will catch up. Don't forget to make a genuine effort to explain Ur vision to Ur followers because leaping ahead without explaining Ur vision is not an effective leadership style either. When U have Rock solid mental strength then stay the course and keep moving forward.

★ **Focus on Details** – When U pay attention to details in any task U undertake, U R Proactively defending against errors. This is a classic step to take in all situations. Every small detail is always important. Like the old saying, no matter how long a chain is, the most important link in any chain is the "*loose link*".

Sometimes when dealing with complicated tasks, Ur mind can get burned out or overworked, and this is when U tend to make mistakes because U lose focus. This is when Ur skills at paying **attention to details** comes into play. It is a **learnable skill** and very valuable and useful too. If U plan your course ahead of time and leave room for every possible contingency, then Ur chances of succeeding also become better.

★ **Be Kind** – Do this in response to anyone and anything U deal with. If someone treats U wrongly, U can either stand Ur ground and greet them Kindly or U can stoop down to their level and act Despicably. While the choice is Urs to make, the outcome may not be what U choose. If U Respond to the wrongdoer the same way they treated U, the level of satisfaction U get or the instant gratification from Ur action may be very tempting, but overall the results of Ur action will be very shameful.

ProAct, ReAct or Respond

When U have a high level of mental strength then petty actions from others shud not drag U down. **Be Nice and Kind to Even** those who mistreat U. U may find that it instills good values in them. Force them to think and earn their respect for being more mature than them. Just Be Kind – Everyone is fighting an inner battle of their own that others have no clue about. **Respond** to other people's problems with a Kind heart. Sometimes all they want is a listening ear. Be unafraid to speak up when it is Ur turn to speak. React to other people's Successes with an open heart – **be Genuine**. Being truthful in Ur words and action is a sign of Integrity in all human interactions.

★ **Be Accountable** – Always be Accountable for Ur actions. This is a very desirable skill for everyone in all levels of life. When U undertake a task of some importance and say U made a huge mistake, it is wise to accept the mistake. Hold Urself responsible, even when making an excuse is an option. When U act responsible like this, U R not only demonstrating that Ur actions are accounted for but also that U R a person of Integrity – a person who cares more about the Result than Ur own image and ego. People always tend to remember how U handled a crisis situation rather than how U got to the crisis in the first place.

★ **Making the Choice** – Decide whether to ProAct, ReAct or Respond to a situation, depending on Ur level of knowledge and maturity. If U R ProActive enough in every task U undertake, U will almost always have contingency plans. So U barely have to ReAct to a situation because almost all the scenarios that can happen have already been assessed and planned for. This is an ideal blueprint for Success. But Real Life is full of surprises. Be mentally Strong and try to Respond positively.

34   **360 Degrees of Life**

★ ***Welcome Changes*** – As someone once said, Nothing in this world is Permanent, Except Change. Always embrace Change. Unless U evolve around a problem, U are not getting better or moving ahead in life. Try to stay positive and respond Happily to the events in Ur life because if its a favorable situation its giving U a memory to hold and if it's unfavorable its giving U an opportunity to learn from it.

What Life has to offer U for Ur future will always be a mystery that makes this Life so **Thrilling**. So why not spend less time worrying about the future and more time planning Ur steps to fulfill Ur vision?? When things change along the way, **Respond** by being flexible – a process simply called ***evolving*** – because historically anything that has resisted evolving has always been erased by time.

When Life pushes U over or pushes U down, be strong, push back ***harder***, jump back up ***faster***, and keep moving ahead in the direction U planned. U have Ur vision and when the vision is clear, don't take Ur eyes Off of it. When U take Ur eyes off Ur Life's Vision, U get distracted by the obstacles along the way. **Keep Ur Focus – Stay Ur course**.

ProAct, ReAct or Respond

Rushing to Judgment

Ur Thoughts can be easily influenced almost instantaneously based on circumstances. There was once a man hiking thru the woods along a trail. After a few hours and a few miles under his belt, he had run out of water or anything else for hydration. He was getting weary and tired. He found a nice shaded area where he decided to take a break before continuing the hike along the trail. He sure was tired, but then he was getting dehydrated too. The wind sure felt good to him, but it did not help with the dehydration.

As he was getting weaker he heard some sound along the trail, and it was approaching towards where he was sitting under the shaded tree. To his pleasant surprise, it was the park ranger making his usual rounds. The ranger asked the man, "Are U Ok?" and wearily the man replied, "Not really, I did not plan this hike out properly, and I have run out of water or anything to keep me hydrated for the rest of the way." Taking pity on the weary hiker, the ranger said, "If U can wait a few minutes right here, I can take this load of logs back to the ranger station and bring back some water for U." The man happily accepted the offer, not like he had much of a choice anyway. Then the man formed **Opinion 1–**
"Wow that ranger is such a nice man; he didn't have to go do that for me."

36   360 Degrees of Life

Minutes went by, almost 15-20 minutes with No sign of the Ranger with the water. Then the man formed **Opinion 2** – "Wow that ranger, gave me false hope and probably forgot about me already." Now the hiker was getting more upset and more tired because he was thinking that not a soul cared for him. Just as he laid his head down in despair, he heard that friendly sound – the sound of the ranger's vehicle. A new ray of hope shined upon the hiker, suddenly he felt more hopeful. Sure enough it was the ranger.

The ranger came to the hiker and said, "I am sorry it took me so long, I knew U were almost dehydrated so I wanted to make a quick lemonade for U – just to get U some electrolytes as well." Then the man formed **Opinion 3** – "Wow the ranger is a nice man after all. He is caring and thoughtful enough that he actually did the extra work to make sure I got electrolytes." The man profusely thanked the Ranger for his thoughtfulness, and before the ranger could utter a word, he poured himself a glass of lemonade and took a big Gulp of the freshly made lemonade. He swallowed it with great difficulty as he was disgusted with the tartness. Then the man formed **Opinion 4** – "Who makes lemonades like this for anyone? This Ranger must be so inconsiderate of other people's taste."

Looking at the hiker's facial expression, the ranger suddenly realized what was happening there. The Ranger said, "I did not get a chance to tell U that I had not added sugar in the lemonade because I did not know whether U are diabetic, and I did not know how much sugar U prefer in Ur lemonade. So here are some sugar packets I brought for U, and here is a spoon to stir it." Then the Man formed **Opinion 5** – "Oh My! This Ranger is an amazing person. He cares for me so much that he was concerned about my taste preference too."

As U can see, it is a very normal scenario that happened in the Hiker and Ranger story. Within a short span of probably less than 1 Hour time, the Hiker had formed 5 distinctly different Opinions about the Ranger, whom he had never met or known

ProAct, ReAct or Respond

before. Neither of the individuals had any impact on each other Outside of that scenario, so it was harmless to both.

Now imagine the same scenario, but the characters are different. One is U, and one is someone U work with, someone who Teaches U, someone who just moved into Ur neighborhood, someone who joined Ur Club or Team or Organization. How wud U **ReAct** or **Respond** to them? Ur Actions are Always going to be aligned with the Opinions U form of the person that U R dealing with. So Be Very CAREFUL while forming Opinions of Others. Do Not Jump to conclusions before analyzing the whole situation from both sides – Ur side and the other person's side. U can never form a Fair Opinion about another person without first knowing them and their situations. So always **Respond** to another person Nicely. Ur Kindness will never go to waste.

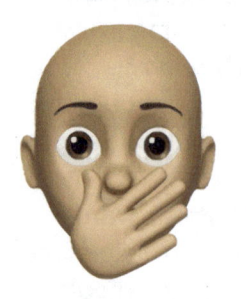

How U treat others will say a Lot about **U**, **Ur Beliefs and Ethics**. Be Nice and Kind to everyone U meet and deal with because Everyone is going through some situations in their life, some battles about which U may have no clue. How U React or Respond to Others can make a huge positive impact on their Life, and sometimes, it can alter the course of their Thoughts and Actions. Try and be a positive impact for anyone that comes in contact with U. There is a beautiful saying about Ur thoughts and vibes – **Ur Vibe attracts Ur Tribe**; so make sure U have Good Vibes all along.

Speaking of Good Vibes, a Leader's contribution to and influence on a team is invaluable. Every Team needs a **Leader** like a vehicle needs a **steering device**, and a Leader is almost meaningless without

360 Degrees of Life

their team just like a steering wheel is pointless without something to steer. The team never belongs to the leader, but the leader belongs to the team. The Team's attitude shud be a reflection of the leader's mindset. An Effective leader's mindset shud be to make the best out of each member of the team. A Leader wud support and Develop their team members such that they can stand up to the plate and deliver their best towards the common goal and vision of the team. How the Team **Responds** to the Leader depends on How the Leader treats the Team.

A wise Leader is always **ProActive** to prevent unexpected results. Develop skills and gain experience in Ur chosen field to the point that U can be **ProActive** in any situation. Make it a habit to be ProActive in Ur general disposition as it will demonstrate that U R able and can effectively Lead because U plan ahead and plan for contingencies too. Always follow Ur Heart, but remember to take Ur Brains with U. If U Only think with Ur Heart, U will not React or Respond to a scenario in the most sensible form. Choices made purely by following Ur Heart tend to be Emotional decisions and U shud know that Emotional Decisions R not always the smartest decisions. Any Effective leader will always try to combine the best of both mental and emotional Choices for the best of the group.

How weird is this??!! People will fall in Love with Strangers after just 1 meeting while Hatred is Usually pointed towards someone whom U have known over a long period of time. It is very hard to Hate someone at first sight, unless U R a judgmental person. If U habitually judge others, U will have a very tough time Living comfortably in society. Humans are Social animals and we Need interactions with Others to be able to Live Happily and comfortably. If U bring in Judgment into every interaction, then U will have a tough time navigating thru Life.

ProAct, ReAct or Respond

I think I Shud ACT like this ...

Define Ur Success and Happiness

Define Ur Success and Happiness
Don't let someone else define it 4 U.

One of the definitions of success I heard many years ago stuck with me – Success is defined as **maximizing** Ur skills and **potentials** so that U can achieve worthwhile objectives and enjoy **some** of the things that money Will buy but **ALL** of the things that money won't buy. There is NO key or miracle or secret to success. However, U can set in motion the key elements that constitute success and happiness in Ur life.

Another measure of Success is that U R happy and healthy, reasonably prosperous, have loving and meaningful relationships and have the hope that the future is going to be even better. This was the way success was defined by master motivator Zig Ziglar. Ur Success shud not be measured by Ur ability to accumulate wealth and material stuff. Instead, it shud be decided by how many people are positively influenced by U and Ur actions and decisions. While U always PLAN for the Future, U gotta always LIVE in the Present because the future depends on the **Choices** U make along the way.

Think of it this way, if U happen to be dying tomorrow, can U say it satisfactorily that Ur life was a success?? Only U can define Ur Success. It may involve a certain amount of financial freedom and friendships among other things. Once U define the vision of Ur success, then get ready to pay the price for it. Success will never come to U accidentally. U gotta work for it and pay the price in terms of time and effort.

The sooner U can define what it means to be Successful and what will make U Happy in life, the faster U will be on track to achieving it. Success is not a destination, it's a journey and a **Way of Life**. Being successful can then become a habit – a habit of producing results without the need of any external motivation.

If U can make a decent living, **doing what U love** to do anyway, then U R unstoppably Successful. Steve Jobs often suggested that "You've got to find what you love. And that is as true for your work as it is for your lovers. Your work is going to fill a large part of your life, and the only way to be truly satisfied is to do what you believe is great work. And the only way to do great work is to love what you do. If you haven't found it yet, keep looking. Don't settle. As with all matters of the heart, you'll know when you find it. And, like any great relationship, it just gets better and better as the years roll on. So keep looking until you find it. Don't settle..." This way U R finding and doing what U love to do, work that gives U mental Satisfaction and Happiness.

If U live each day as if it is Ur last, **someday U will be right**. Keeping that in mind, anytime Ur heart leads U away from your goals, ask yourself, "If it were my last day would I be wasting it doing this...??" The answer to it shud bring U right back on track. Our lifetime is limited, so V shud not waste it living someone else's plan. Be brave, take risks, follow Ur Dreams. Even if U fail, sooner or later U will get a result that Ur heart truly desires and U have worked for.

Remember to always celebrate Ur successes, no matter how small they are. Ur success is Urs to recognize. Don't let others judge them. When U celebrate Ur Successes, U feel motivated to achieve more results like it, and pretty soon U get into the Habit of making Successful Choices and Decisions.

Define Ur Success and Happiness

What is Success ??

Here are some ways to look at Success at different ages:

- ★ When U R 18 months Old, U R successful if U can stand up on Ur own.
- ★ At age 8 U R successful if U R able to ride bicycle without training wheels.
- ★ At age 18 U R successful if U R able go to the college of Ur Choice.
- ★ At age 28 U R successful if U R able to start a family of Ur own.
- ★ At age 38 U R successful if U R able to maintain a family structure of Ur own.
- ★ At age 58 U R successful if U R able to guide Ur children to a meaningful career.
- ★ At age 68 U R successful if U R able to live a comfortable retired life.
- ★ At age 88 U R successful if U R able to walk without any support...

And so the story of life and social definitions of successes goes on. Remember NONE of the above things has any actual value unless U give meaning to it. It is Ur definition of success at any stage of life that matters, NOT what others think about it.

Have Visions 'n' Dreams

It is always **Easier** to climb the ladder of success when U separate Urself from the crowd at the bottom. U wanna hang around with people who have **visions** and **dreams**. Together U can put Ur skills to use and help each other to a whole new level of achievement. The first step is to fix that vision of Ur Future clearly in Ur mind. From there create Ur own goals program. U know Ur strengths and weakness, so U R the best person to set Ur own goals. **Set small achievable goals** first and then gradually move on to bigger and harder goals. Ur goals can be as small as including a vegetable in every meal of the day to start *getting Urself healthier*.

360 Degrees of Life

Ur goals does not have to be super complicated. Keep it **Simple**. Simple is usually usable – complicated is usually interesting but seldom useful. If it is simple enough then U will Do it, if not U can get lost in the complications.

Take the analogy of Soccer/ Football. There are only 3 simple things to do to play the game. U got to **Dribble**, U got to **Pass** and U got to **Shoot**. That's it. So technically speaking, anyone who can master these 3 simple things can play Soccer/ Football and can potentially win the game and be a superstar. Now, how WELL U do those 3 things differentiates the average player from those all time superstars and legends of the game like Messi or Ronaldo or Pele. In reality to become a successful player, some of the key elements required are **Focus** and ability to work as a **Team player**. More often than not, whatever U focus on expands into Ur reality. U must focus on the key things that drive U towards Ur definition of Success. U gotta set the right expectations first. When U R going to play, Expect to win, Expect that Ur whole team will perform at its Best, and then make sure that **U do Ur Best** as well.

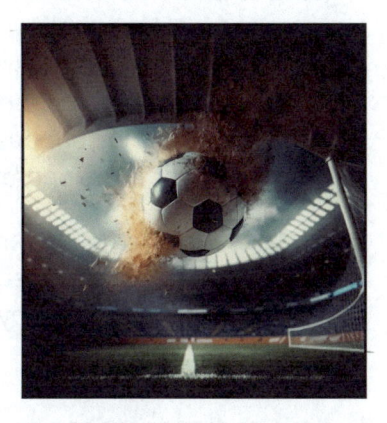

Have Realistic Goals, and work towards them. Winning a game based on Ur team's effort and skills is a realistic goal. Beware of unrealistic goal, eg. winning this one game making U a wealthy sport professional. Don't let anything move Ur Focus away from Ur Goals and Vision. Most of the time when U R motivated well enough to Succeed and be Happy, U need to plan to work towards these goals. Remember Success and Happiness are not destinations, they are parts of a *journey*, a *lifestyle*.

Once Ur goals, and visions of Success are determined, then U gotta work whenever and however long it takes, not because U love to work like crazy machines, but because that is the need of the hour and that is the driving force that is going to launch U into that next stage in ur journey. Don't let anyone fool U into believing that being successful is easy. If people try, one of 3 things is happening. Either they are lying or they have already done the hard parts of their success journey, so now being successful is easy for them, or they know a whole lot more secrets to success than anyone else.

Being successful is never easy, it is NO stroll in the park – it takes every ounce of Ur energy. That is IF U want to play big and be successful and happy.

Standards of Success

It is misleading to judge success by simple appearance. Ur clothes or Ur friends shud not define Ur success. U never know what someone has defined for their own success, because in Ur opinion they may appear to be not successful.

Before trying to become a Successful person, try to become a **Good Person**, because Success may come and go, but a Good name always stays – even after U R long gone. Ur wins R Urs – U own them. However they may not be of interest to another person. Like the old saying, one man's treasure is another man's trash. Nobody's gotta lose in order for U to win either – except in games.

Too often, people do not have a problem achieving their goals, the real problem is they set their goals pretty low and hit them. Instead set Ur goals higher. Even if U miss them, U R at least on a higher ground than where U started off. So RAISE Ur Standards and Expectations, so U are always aiming for a higher ground.

Ur Success

Yes, Ur Success is Urs alone and gratifying to U. And that Success becomes more meaningful when it is reflected thru the eyes of someone that believed in U all the while – it could be Ur parents, Ur relatives or that Uncle/Aunt that always believed in U or that friend who has always been there and believed in Ur abilities.

So always try to have a few sincere relationships in Ur Life – relationships where nothing is expected and everything matters. Because once U have defined Ur Success and Ur happiness factors, the next most important thing to have in Life is someone to share it with, otherwise everything will seem meaningless at the end of Ur journey.

Listen to what Others have to say but DO what U believe is Right because only U know what works for U. U hold the personal remote controller for Ur Life, don't let someone or something else control U. DO what Inspires U and don't fall into the Ambition trap. Keep it real and always remember the Power of Pride – Take Pride in anything U do. The satisfaction U get is totally worth it.

There is a beautiful poem written by the English novelist of *Jungle Book* fame, Rudyard Kipling. This poem is from *Rewards and Fairies* from back in 1910. It is a nice message from a father figure to his son but can be adopted into much more than that. Here's a glimpse of the original version: (*highlighting the parts I want U to emphasize*)

> If you can keep your head when all about you
> Are losing theirs and blaming it on you;
> If you can **trust yourself when all men doubt you**,
> But make allowance for their doubting too:
> If you can wait and not be tired by waiting,

Or being lied about, don't deal in lies,
Or being hated don't give way to hating,
And yet don't look too good, nor talk too wise;

If you can **dream—and not make dreams your master**;
If you can think—and not make thoughts your aim,
If you can meet with Triumph and Disaster
And treat those two impostors just the same:
If you can bear to hear the truth you've spoken
Twisted by knaves to make a trap for fools,
Or watch the things you gave your life to, broken,
And stoop and build 'em up with worn-out tools;

If you can make one heap of all your winnings
And risk it on one turn of pitch-and-toss, And lose,
and start again at your beginnings
And never breathe a word about your loss:
If you can force your heart and nerve and sinew
To serve your turn long after they are gone,
And so hold on when there is nothing in you
Except the Will which says to them: 'Hold on!'

If you can **talk with crowds and keep your virtue**,
Or walk with Kings—nor lose the common touch,
If neither foes nor loving friends can hurt you,
If all men count with you, but none too much:
If you can fill the unforgiving minute
With sixty seconds' worth of distance run,
Yours is the Earth and everything that's in it,
And—which is more—you'll be a Man, my son!

This is a very beautifully crafted poem, profound and self-explanatory (*emphasis mine*).

Successful Lifestyle

A successful lifestyle can have certain key ingredients, one version of it may be shown as below:

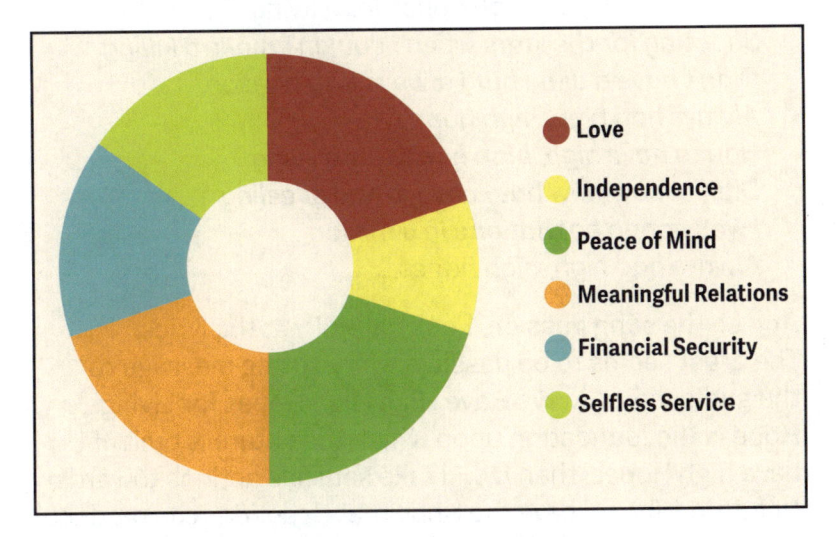

- Love
- Independence
- Peace of Mind
- Meaningful Relations
- Financial Security
- Selfless Service

The above depiction is One Version depending on One viewpoint. Different individuals will have different breakdowns for each of these categories. For some people the feeling of Loving Someone and Being Loved is perhaps far more important than the sense of Independence while for someone else Peace of Mind will be a top priority. U choose how U want to look at it, U gotta define what U want for Ur life.

When it comes to happiness, usually it depends on something happening around U. If they R not giving U the sense of happiness then U have two choices. Either U change Ur situation or U change Ur attitude towards the situation. This way, ultimately Ur happiness ends up in Ur hands. A popular song from 2018 which received several awards including the 2019 Billboard Music Award and 2019 MTV Video music award for Top Rock Song was a song called **"High Hopes"**, by Panic! At The Disco, from the album Pray for the Wicked. The song has very motivational lyrics that might interest some of U, here are a few lines from the song:

> Had to have high, high hopes for a living
> Shooting for the stars when I couldn't make a killing
> Didn't have a dime but I always had a vision
> Always had high, high hopes
> Had to have high, high hopes for a living
> Didn't know how but I always had a feeling
> I was gonna be that one in a million
> Always had high, high hopes…

And so the song goes on. Look carefully at the lyrics. The artist seems to be passing a very strong message to the audience – Always Have High High Hopes for Living…. Hope is the foundation upon which the Future is built. If U have high Hopes, then U will take sensible actions towards Ur future. When U have the Hope that Ur actions can produce positive results in Ur life, building a better future for Urself, then U will automatically perform better and be accountable for Ur actions.

Happiness Factors

Ur Happiness can be directly affected by the following 4 factors:

★ The Exercises you do to strengthen Ur body
★ The Services U do for others
★ The Social interactions U have with others
★ The Recognitions U get from others.

Each of the above 4 factors has totally different chemical stimulations in Ur brain. The so-called Happiness inducing hormones like **Endorphin**, **Dopamine**, **Serotonin** and **Oxytocin** are released based on different physical actions, and each of them has a very positive influence on Ur overall mood that V title as "Happiness."

Endorphin

Dopamine

Serotonin

Oxytocin

For instance, we know for a fact that Oxytocin is responsible for the nice warm, affectionate feelings U have when someone treats U nicely. When U do something nice for someone or someone does something nice for U, an abundance of oxytocin is produced in Ur body giving U that happy feeling. The funny thing is when U see someone doing some selfless deed for another person, just witnessing the act gives U some pleasure and a sense of happiness on a different level. Even in this scenario oxytocin is the secret agent behind it. U can even say that the very purpose of oxytocin is to preserve this beautiful, unselfish feeling of mutual happiness among humans.

Humans are more or less like cars. If U want a car to operate you've got to refuel it, whether it be with petroleum products or an electric charge or whatever else may be the energy source. For us humans, these energy sources are often things that motivate us, things that give us joy and happiness. Just like cars, we need to get refueled regularly, and we do that by engaging in activities that give us the feeling of being re-energized and refueled.

Some feel revitalized by doing physical exercise, while for others it may be by engaging in some volunteer work. Whatever it is that makes U Happy and excited, **Do It** ! If that activity is of use to other humans, some might say that's even better. U decide.

Linguists have found out that there are a LOT more words to describe specific unhappy events as opposed to happy events. Leo Tolstoy, in one of his novels, said that every Happy Family

Define Ur Success and Happiness

is similar while every Unhappy family is going through a different scenario. In a lot of ways it still holds true, because in general for people to be happy, there are a few key ingredients that constitute what V all perceive as happiness while unhappiness can be caused by a variety of issues.

Lot of times, V tend to dwell on our unhappy situations and that often leads to more complex problems like depression and anxiety. Instead if V shift our focus to the good and positive events of our days and life in general, then our mind will say, "give me more." This way being happy and staying happy becomes a part of Ur demeanor, and U attract more and more things that will keep U happy and support Ur mental health as well.

Misconceptions on Success and Happiness

It is a common misconception that we have to always Move Forward in order to Succeed. Here's a classic example from a game which most of U R familiar with: In the standard **Tug of War** as shown, V all know it well that we need to step backward in order to Succeed in this game. Similarly, nowhere is it defined that in order for U to succeed in any situation U need to always move ahead, sometimes in Life we need to take a step backward, or sometimes even a few steps backward to get our direction aligned for Success.

52   360 DEGREES of Life

Except for sporting scenarios, nowhere in real life is there a Need to Defeat someone in order to Succeed. Remember, Ur definition of Success is Urs, and it is relative when everything else around it is considered. U do not necessarily have to defeat someone to feel Successful. Building **Ur character** is very critical in defining Ur Success and Happiness too. The importance of Character is so much that it prompted someone to say, If Wealth is lost **Nothing** is lost (it can be earned back). If Health is lost **Something** is lost (it's hard but can be earned back), but when Character is lost **Everything** is lost.

Money = Tool ≠ Goal.

A Lot of people in our society equate Success and Happiness with the amount of Money U have and the Title U hold at work and Ur material possessions. Look at those things again and ask Urself – Is there anything there that is permanent?? **NO**, obviously Not. None of these things are permanent and U did not come into the face of this earth with any of these things either, then why give it all so much importance?? If the amount of Money U have determines Ur Happiness then let me ask U – **How much Money is Enough**?? How much Money do U NEED to Have before U can say that "I have Enough Now."?? Or are U stuck in a Vicious Cycle of dissatisfaction because U really don't know how much Money is Enough, so U are running the rat race with everyone else with no breaks and No clue what U R running for??

If U stop and think at some point in life and U R not able to define what U R running for, then U know for a fact that Ur running for the wrong stuff, the meaningless stuff. Usually it is a sign for U to change the direction of Ur run and the reasons to run too. A Sad but true fact is that a lot of people run aimlessly like the rats in the rat race – because of a lack of vision. To get out of that cycle, all U have to do is to Define Ur Success and Happiness factors. Give Value to things in Life which R actually worthwhile.

Define Ur Success and Happiness

U can have all the material possessions U desire and still feel very empty and very dissatisfied because after U pass thru what people normally called the Toy Stage of Success, pretty soon U realize that the things that U actually Enjoy in Life don't cost a whole lot of money and no amount of STUFF is going to make U any more happier than U decide to be. Pretty soon all those possessions start losing their value in Ur own eyes as well. So make sure to Choose the Right things when U define Ur Success and Happiness. That is one of the Foundation Slabs for Ur long lasting Satisfied Lifestyle.

If money isn't the route to Happiness, what is??
Baden Powell, the founder of the Scouting movement, maintained that the real way to get happiness is by giving out happiness to other people.

This is How I define my Success and Happiness...

Define Ur Success and Happiness

What's Ur Motivation??

What's Ur Motivation??

What gets U up and going ??!!

There must be something in life that would get Ur ... Up and Going. What is that?? That's what you have to identify. For U to be able to define that, first U must be able to do what's been talked about in the previous chapter – *Define Ur Success and Happiness*. Once U have determined what Success means to U personally, then U will know what gets U going.

Pain and **Pleasure** are the 2 main motivators for humans. For some, the **Pleasure** of Success is the prime **motivator**, while for others, the **Pain** of Failure is their motivator. A lot of times people claim that motivation is temporary – if you stretch that point a bit, so is bathing and eating. Now U and I both know for a fact that if U keep continuing to eat in an appropriate healthy manner, then Ur chances of living R infinitely more than not eating anything at all. In the same way, if U find Ur motivators, they will help U keep moving in the right direction in life.

A few of the **common motivators** for people R hunger, gaining a better lifestyle, accumulation of wealth, improvement in health, and finding newer opportunities to make a living. Some motivators are **more significant and selfless** like making a positive impact in the society, being useful to the needy, making hefty contributions to the welfare of mankind, imparting knowledge to the masses and the list goes on. Each person must discover their own motivator – they are as different as the individuals themselves.

Since the beginning of recorded time, humans have been involved in some type of a rat race, seeking personal gains. For the longest time, the race was for mere survival, then it became

360 Degrees of Life

a race for control over others, for control over land, for control over natural resources and so on. Energy and resources spent in making those personal gains will prove futile if they do not follow with a bigger and more **meaningful purpose** in life. It is sad to know that there are many self-centered people in our society today who consider volunteering as a waste of time. They don't understand that the joy U get in doing a good deed for another living being can never be experienced through any material possessions.

"It is very hard (to contribute) more than you consume. To **try to have a positive net contribution to society**, I think that's the thing to aim for," Elon Musk of Tesla fame said in a 2021 podcast (emphasis mine). Thoughts along these lines are very important because ever since the character-based education system has been fading away from our society, we have been dealing with more and more self-centered individuals. Once they start to outnumber the generous, the kind and the people with a serving mentality, our society will be in great danger of its very existence. Since the days of the barter system, Human society was formed on the fundamental principle of **give and take**, Not just Take.

Dare to Dream, and don't just dream to "make a living", dream bigger, dream to make a positive difference around U. Ur Dream MUST be followed by an action plan. Dreams without a follow-up action are just Wishes. A **Wish** is nothing but a hope for something over which U have no control. A **Dream**, on the other hand, is a vision U have.

Some parts of Science have proven that humans don't dream in color. Even if people claim they dream in color most of them cannot remember what colors they saw in their dream etc. 90-95% of the information U see in a dream is not retained

What's Ur Motivation??

right after U R awake. I say, give color and wings to Ur dreams. Elaborate Ur dreams. Make Ur dreams SO **colorful** and powerful that they keep U awake and motivated all the time. I'm talking about the Dreams U see with Ur eyes open – the Dangerous ones. They are the Visions, the visions of a future with a purpose.

Earl Nightingale said, "Never give up on a dream just because of the length of time it will take to accomplish it." When it comes to chasing Ur dreams, **do whatever it takes** to achieve it, whatever that is **Legal**, **Moral** and **Ethical** of course, and do not fret about the time it might take to achieve that dream. Any dream, big or small, is like making a structure from building blocks; U've got to build it one block at a time.

Just like a kid building a structure with blocks by looking at a picture, U got to have Ur vision in mind, and then every step U take should get U one step closer to the fulfillment of that vision. A dream is more easily realized if Ur life is in **perfect balance** and U have a clear vision of what U want to achieve.

What does it mean to have a Life in perfect balance?? When U R at school, U should be only concentrating on Ur studies. When U R at work U should be only focusing on the projects going on at work. When U R at home U should be concentrating on tending to the needs of Ur family. This habit of dividing up Ur time and focus will help U go long ways in life, keeping things in Balance.

360 Degrees of Life

Here are some other 🗝 to achieving Ur goals:

No matter what U R doing or where U R performing, always make it a point to give it Ur **absolute Best** every single time. How U motivate Urself is mostly dependent on how big Ur ambitions and dreams are. Setting proper life goals is very keen to Ur own personal growth. By proper goals, I mean, don't set a goal that is SO high that in Ur own mind U R saying, "This ain't happening." The goals U set shud be **well defined** and **practical** to the point that the only thing between U and Ur goals shud be Ur efforts and a reasonable amount of time.

🗝 All Ur actions must be **accountable**. U must take responsibilities for Ur actions. This is a significant **step** toward a prudent lifestyle. Being prudent means making wise decisions based on some basic principles you believe in and then managing your practical life choices in a shrewd and discreet manner. For example, U can hold Urself responsible for being the role model for those around U and stand up to **Say No to Drugs**; it takes a lot of **courage** to stand out in a crowd. Studies have shown that people who lead a more prudent life can also end up having a longer, healthier life than the carefree and happy-go-lucky sorts.[3] The study also showed that Hard working people who advanced in their careers and took on more responsibility were also more likely to live long, healthy lives.[4]

🗝 **Persistence**. Don't stop until U reach Ur goal. Dream big and have the vision, but then break it down into smaller goals, Goals U can achieve in stages. As U achieve them one by one, U will feel more and more confident and comfortable because U will realize that what U R doing is building some solid foundations towards that Bigger vision U have set for Urself.

What's Ur Motivation??

Ur vision may be to become the best in some field, some sport or skill which U think is cool and U think U can make a living at, While enjoying the activity as well. Remember the first few times U engage in that activity, U may find it to be much more challenging than it appeared to be, but remember the 🗝 is not to give up, to keep trying to get better at it. Remember every master was once a disaster. Everything U want to do U can, as long as U understand that the people U see as models were once terrible at it too. The only way to better Urself is through Experience and Education.

🗝 ***Perspective***. U have heard, "Its Not what U say – but How U say that matters", right?? In life it is How U See things that is more important than what U see. In a truly entrepreneurial experience, anything that U see and perceive as a problem is nothing more than an ***opportunity***. An opportunity where U can create a solution – a solution to the needs of another person. Finding solutions to another's need and making a living at it can simply be termed as ***Basics of Business***. Helping a person in need is different from business, because in business we provide the service or solution to the problem for a ***profit***. However, helping a person might trigger an idea for a Business opportunity.

🗝 Ur ***Imagination*** comes in very handy at this point. Finding a solution to a commonly occurring problem and then finding a business model for this solution requires some wild ***imagination*** – systematic ***planning***, and ***follow through***. For a series of events like this to happen, U need to open the blinds in Ur minds like a kid looking thru a window to the world outside. Ur mind performs at its best when it is Fully open.

360 Degrees of Life

For those who are on the way to success, difficulties are often a part of **their lives**, while for those who have succeeded, difficulties are often a part of **their life story**. So the journey between Ur present day and Ur vision for future is very critical. Don't ever loose Ur Focus on Ur vision. There are always going to be diversions and detours, but as long as U maintain the course, U R sure to reach Ur destination. Ur vision for future shud be Ur primary motivator.

Progress. Try *doing* a simple "connect the dots" puzzle, U will see that U have to constantly look back before moving forward to the next dot to make sure that the newer connections combined with the older ones are actually making some sense. It's the same way in life. U need to look back – back in time – to see each of those connections U made in the past. Then U will start seeing a clearer picture of where Ur actions are leading U. If they R in line with Ur vision of Ur future then U know all U have to do is to believe Ur heart and keep moving in that direction.

Confucius said, "It does not matter how slowly you go so long as you do not stop." No matter what obstacles U face, keep moving forward at Ur own pace, this is the only way U can make progress in Life. **Steve Jobs** of Apple fame always inspired by saying, keep moving forward in the direction of Ur beliefs. Jobs used to say, whatever is the guiding light for U, Ur gut, destiny or karma, ***Follow It***. This is the only way U will have the confidence to move on, even when U move away from the well-worn path and that is what will make all the difference.

Hope!! If U R ever feeling helpless, Start believing in the power of Hope. The world revolves around the power of hope,

What's Ur Motivation??

without hope there is no future. Life may not always be easy, **particularly at Ur Stage**, but when U overcome that tough, rough spot, U will understand that it was all well worth it. Usually, every Scenario U deal with will either be an enjoyable experience or an experiential teacher. If U think about it carefully, U got nothing to lose. Either way U are gaining something towards Ur life.

🗝️ **Head 'n' Heart**. Science has proved that V R moved **emotionally** by what V hear and **logically** by what V see. So it is very important that V hear the right things, stuff that will motivate us in the right direction towards our vision for the future. When V make sure that V hear the right things, our mind will be set in the right direction. When our thoughts R in the right direction, then V know our actions that follow those thoughts R also going to be in the right direction. Ur Thoughts lead to Ur Actions which lead to Ur Results. So when U have Ur thoughts and Ur actions aligned with Ur vision U will definitely achieve Ur desired results.

🗝️ **Motivators**. Just like Pain and Pleasure, another big motivator in life is **Hunger**, which can be considered a subset of pain. Hunger is a prime motivator for almost all of the animal kingdom. I don't think most animals hunt for fun but rather to satisfy their hunger. Their hunger makes them attracted to the bait of the hunter. If there were NO Hunger, no birds or animals would ever fall into a hunter's net. U can have hunger for a good quality of life, or for better health and so on. Just make sure Ur not overly hungry for power or wealth, things that can often lead U into destruction.

If U Cannot Fight for What U Want, Don't Cry for What U Lost.

360 Degrees of Life

Risk It!! Anything U do or want to do depends on some form of motivators. The risk associated with it becomes a measuring factor that determines how badly U want the results. Finally this lets U take the most important step in the whole process, **Action**. In my opinion, if there is even a small chance that doing something or achieving something Might make U happy, then go ahead and ***Risk It*** – it's All Worth It. At this point don't let someone fool U into believing something against it, and definitely don't let Ur self-limiting beliefs stop U either.

S.M.A.R.T. Any Goals U set shud have a few inherent features. Like they R taught in the Scouting world, Every Goal U set in Life Shud be a **S.M.A.R.T. Goal**. The acronym stands for Specific, Measurable, Attainable, Relevant and Timely. This is very critical for any Goals U set in life. The more Specific Ur goals, the easier it becomes to identify the details and make Choices towards the Goals. Every Goal U set should be Measurable and Attainable. Measurable means U can actually see Ur progress to the End. Attainable means it is of a size that allows U to get there. Attainable simply means, don't make Ur Goals to build a castle in the air. Set Realistic expectations for Urself. Ur goals Shud be Relevant to Ur Vision of Future. Every step U take by setting up smaller Goals Shud move U towards Ur final vision. Timeliness is very important, because A Goal without a Timeline and Action plan is just a Wish.

Whatever be Ur Motivation to perform in Life, always remember, U R rewarded in public for all the practice and hard work U do in private. Like in any professional sport, the player's 1-2 hours of peak performance is often backed by hours or months, sometimes even years, of hard-core practice.

What's Ur Motivation??

What's Ur Motivation??

Back in 2009, **Usain Bolt** became the fastest human recorded and alive at the time. He did not just show up at the 100-meter sprint and cover it in 9.58 seconds, the 1st time he ran it, nor the 2nd time he tried it, probably not even the 100th time. He must have trained and planned for years before he set records on the world stage.

It is Motivation that drives people to perform at their Best. People usually don't start learning a skill unless it interests them. Once U gain interest in a skill, enjoy it and put time into improving it. U can become the Best at it depending on what price U R willing to pay, in terms of **Time** and **Effort**.

Here's an African proverb that might hit the point. No matter how tall Ur grandfather was, U still have to do Ur own growing. What it means is that, it doesn't matter what Ur background is, U still need to do Ur own Growing and Living.

When U choose Ur motivators, choose the right ones and for the right reasons. Like the proverb pointed, it really doesn't matter what background U come from or what Ur lineage is. U have to create Ur own identity and that begins by having Ur own visions for Ur future.

If U look at Life as a stage, then U can say that here the actors and directors have no clue what is coming up next or what the act is about. To stay in the game of Life, make sure U have some worthwhile goals. Plan and Prepare to work towards Ur Goals every step of the way. This way U R prepared for whatever that comes up. Ur preparation will always depend on Ur Vision and Ur Motivators.

360 Degrees of Life

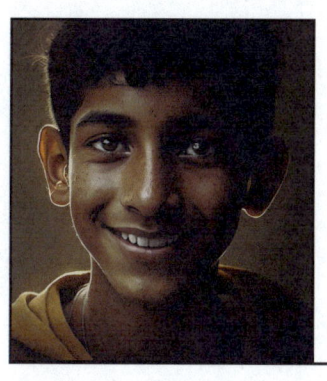

What's Ur Motivation??

What's Ur Motivation??

Choices...

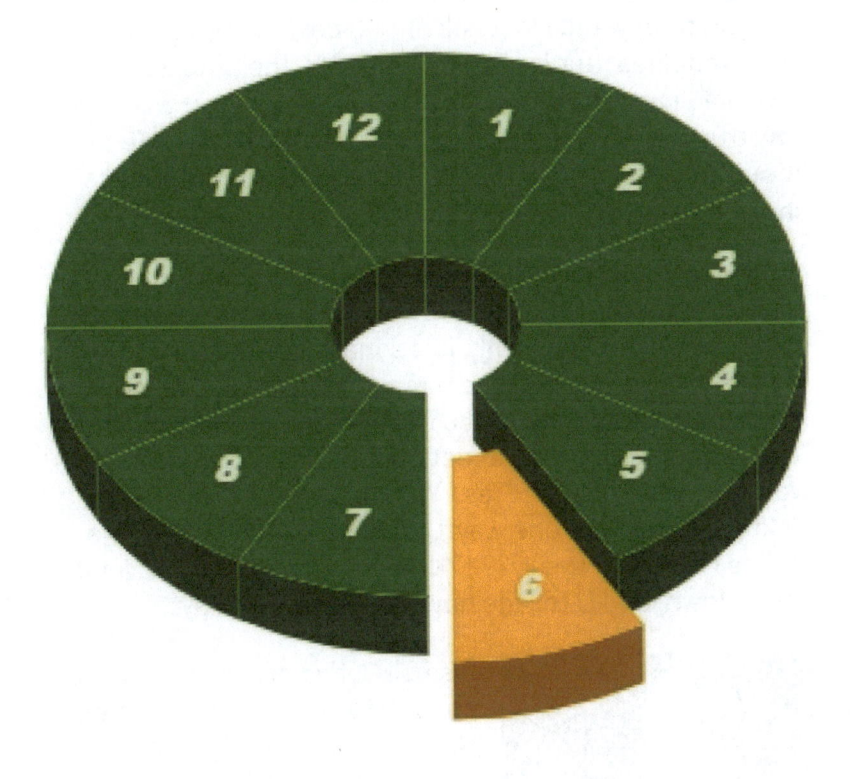

Choices ...

Is it a surprise?? Life is FULL of them.

The secret to Life is All about Choices – from small, insignificant ones to huge life-altering ones. Every choice U make along the journey of life leads U to another choice. Whether U wake up in the morning or whether U want to stay up late at night, Ur day and life R Full of Choices. At any given time, Ur current life situation is a result of ALL the Choices you have made up until then – read that again and you will know how true that is. Some choices can change every little thing about Ur life and every moment thereafter. While some choices are trivial like the size of Ur morning coffee.

Nelson Mandela said, "There is no passion to be found playing small and settling for a life less than the one you are capable of living." Basically, it is a message to wake U to the reality that the Choices U make in life should always be focussed on bringing out the Best in You. Now U may ask, "Do all Choices have an effect on my Life?" A simple one word answer would be "Yes." Yes it makes a difference in Ur life in more than one way. U might ask, "The size of the Coffee I order??!! Really??!!" Now read that again and let it settle down, and U tell me how it will affect Ur day.

A small Coffee might give U a boost enough to wake U up and sharpen Ur senses temporarily. The amount of sweetener U add will give it a whole new spin. If U decided to get a large cup of coffee instead and U consume it fully in a short period of time, U might get ultra active for a short period of time and then fade out as the effect of that external motivator, Caffeine, in this case wears out. So U see, every decision U make, every

Choice U make has some effect on U directly or indirectly, visibly or otherwise. This is why I urge that where there R Choices to be made, always make the ones you won't regret.

U can identify Urself as one of the following 4 types of people:

1. VICTIMS
Blame everything around themselves for things they have no control over. Everything ends up being a problem, and the whole world is working against them. They are always looking for a savior to come rescue them from their problems.

2. INFO ADDICTS
They R never ready to take any Action. They feel they don't have just enough information to do what needs to be done, and they always feel insecure or scared that they R not fully prepared to take the endeavor whatever that might be.

3. PERFORMERS
They actually get things done. These R the people who move mountains, form teams and make effective changes in the society.

4. EXISTENTS
They just exist on the face of the earth. They R the unmotivated ones who have nothing defined for themselves. They act as rebels but R almost nonexistent to anyone around them. They don't affect anyone or anything except maybe annoy the Performers.

Life. **The Choice** is Urs. If U want to make a positive impact around U then U need to become a **Performer**. If U see a problem, U shud tackle it to the best of Ur abilities. If the problem is beyond Ur control but U believe that it is solvable then find resources to tackle it. If it is not solvable, be mature and deal with it. There are things in this life which we have to

Choices...

just deal with – the simplest example wud be aging. U can Age Gracefully or Grumpy – it is definitely a Choice.

It really doesn't matter what Ur past has been, it does not matter what Ur present situation is either. What really matters is, there is **something specific** that U can do NOW which will definitely alter the course of Ur future, and the **Choice is Urs** to make. So make wise **Choices**. Each one of us can make some Choices that can either build or break our path to our future.

When U were a kid, depending on Ur physical attributes, strengths and weaknesses U were taught how to perform basic activities – from walking to talking, reading and so forth. As U grew older, U actually had to decide to do them Urself. Others can teach U how to talk, U have to do the talking Urself. Ur teachers can teach U how to read, U have to do the reading. Basically, U can get all the help U need in life, but nothing happens unless **U choose to perform**. As with a driver and the guided navigations from a GPS, the GPS will try to help U navigate towards Ur destination, but U have to follow its directions. A GPS cannot force U to turn or go straight, the choice is Urs.

Choose to be around people who encourage U and see the good in U. Usually V become a part of what V R normally around all the time. If U R around people with **strong positive mental attitude**, then U and Ur thoughts will always be focused on positive

360 Degrees of Life

things in life, things U CAN do and things U CAN affect in a positive way etc. Ur thinking will be good. U never climb the high mountains alone; U always achieve great things in conjunction with other like-minded and encouraging people, so try and surround Urself with the right kind of people.
It is a Choice.

Having a positive mental attitude will not enable U to work miracles, but it will help U perform any task slightly better than if U had approached it with a negative attitude. How U approach a task makes a world of difference on how U handle it. Having a positive attitude does not mean believing that everything will turn out to be OK. Instead it means that **U will be OK** no matter how things turn out. That is a perspective U can adapt to guarantee a calm and focused approach to any issues U might face in Life.

Any task U undertake will seem to be easy if U approach it with the right attitude. For example, if U love to cook, U might say it takes about 20-30 minutes to put together a nice, nourishing meal for two. That is looking at cooking in a positive way because U love to do it.

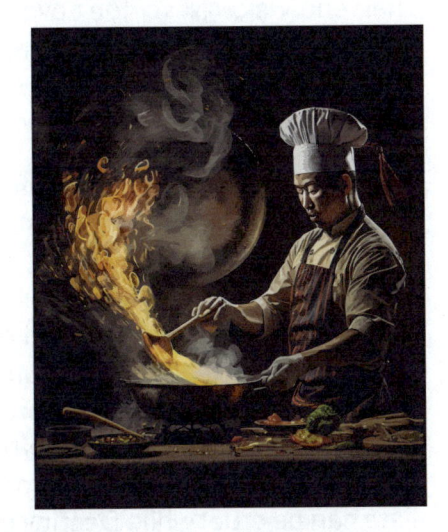

The same task will look like an ordeal if U R not very fond of cooking, now everything related to cooking, from prepping the food to washing dishes will look like big tasks, simply because U don't enjoy the main thing, which is the cooking part. So how U approach a task plays a Huge part in how U perform a task and how well.

Choices...

Live Ur life in Ur own time zone. Some of Ur friends may seem to go ahead of U in life while some may seem to fall behind. That doesn't mean some are better than others. Everyone is running their own race in their own time zones. Just because New York is 5 hours behind London does not mean New York is slower than London. Everyone is ON time in their own time zones and so R U. Don't compare Ur accomplishments with that of another person because they might be working on a completely different time zone of their own.

U may not know where they started their journey and what their end Vision is, so don't ever Fret over a glimpse of what U see from someone's life. There may be more to their story than what meets the eye. Everyone V see is fighting a battle V know nothing about, so no point in comparing.

When talking about Life and Life Choices, U often come across terms like Fate and Destiny. **Fate** usually points to outside forces affecting Ur life, things over which U have no control – Acts of Nature or God if U want to address it that way. Destiny on the other hand refers to the intended future, a future that is shaped based on Ur **Choices**. Which is why it is very commonly said that U create Ur **Destiny**. Destiny depends on the size of Ur **ambitions**, the strength of Ur **desires** and Ur **determination** or willpower to attain them. Fate can be cruel while Destiny can be **Crafted**.

Staying Happy is a Choice. Staying Healthy is a Choice. Staying Positive and Upbeat is a Choice. Being Trustworthy is a Choice. Being Loyal is a Choice. Being Helpful is a Choice. Being Friendly is a Choice. Being Courteous is a Choice. Being Kind is a Choice. Being Obedient is a Choice. Being Financially Savvy is a Choice. Being Brave is a Choice.

360 Degrees of Life

Friendly/Helpful
Trustworthy
Positive/Upbeat
Healthy
Kind/Courteous
Reverent
Obedient
Clean/Honorable
Loyal
Brave/Confident
Financial Savvy
Cheerful/Happy

Choices...

Being Clean is a Choice. Being Respectful is a Choice. When U look at all these together, U realize these are some amazing traits to possess for ANY human being.

Each one of them is a Choice U can make, and these are some of the Qualities they embrace as youths and adults in the world of **Scouting**. Each of these qualities has a great significance in the way Ur journey of Life takes turns for the Good. These are some of the MOST sought after and most admirable qualities one can possess as a Human. If more and more people chose these qualities to live by, our Society wud become a much better place for the future generations.

Here's a quick illustration on Opinions vs. Choices:

75

Choices...

U guessed it right, in either of the scenarios, there will be people to voice their opinion about the old folks and their actions. In the case where they are walking beside the donkey, people might say, "The old folks are foolish, they are not even using the donkey." In the second case where they are both riding the donkey, people might say, "The old folks are being cruel to the donkey." No matter what the old folks choose to do, there will be someone to raise a negative opinion about it.

Remember, people's opinions are theirs to keep and / or share. That does not mean U have to alter Ur actions based only on their opinions. The Choice is Urs, because **U and Only U** know what is the real story behind the scene. What may appear as a foolish choice to a viewer might be the ONLY possible choice for the performer.

The person that is just watching what's happening wud never completely know what the person performing the act is going thru, and that makes the WORLD of difference. So, be very slow to form opinions about other people's actions, because most of the time U don't know the whole story. What appears in front of Ur eyes may in fact be just a tip of the iceberg.

Here's another idea on Perspective:

As we can see clearly, to the woman on the left, this might look like a number "6" while to the man on the right, this might look like a number "9", and they BOTH are **Right** from their OWN perspective. This is a classic scenario where U have to decide what is right and what is wrong based on Ur own perspective. There are No Rights and No Wrongs in most scenarios. It is merely how U interpret the situation based on the information available to U at that moment. It is all fine, as long as the choices U make or the opinions U form are within the realm of what is Legal, Moral and Ethical.

There was once this naughty kid who always did the opposite of what she was told. One day she is running around in the garden and happened to catch a butterfly. She runs up to her mom and says, "If you tell me the answer correctly, I will do whatever task it is that you ask me to do." Mom agrees, so she covers the butterfly inside her palms and asks the mom, "Is the butterfly in my hand dead or alive??" This puts the mom in a difficult spot. The mother explains to the kid. "Remember, its life is in Ur hands because no matter what I say U R gonna do the opposite. So if I say it's alive, U R gonna kill it, and if U have decided to kill it anyway then it's dead too. So ultimately, no matter what I say, the life of that butterfly is in Ur hands." The same way, no matter what anyone says to U, about U, Ur life ultimately depends ONLY on U and Ur choices and actions. Whether U want to make something nice out of Ur life or just waste it away because someone said something that offended U, it is a Choice U have to make. So Choose Wisely. Make Ur Choices not to Prove or Disprove someone but do the right thing, given Ur circumstances.

Usually there are NO rights and NO wrongs; Ur choice usually depends on the viewpoint U take about the situation. In the picture on the left, the number can be viewed as a 6 or a 9. No matter how U look at it, one person is going to be Right and the other is going to be Wrong. But remember actually

Choices...

they BOTH are Right from their own viewpoints, and in the same way, the choices U make in life should be Right in Ur viewpoint, because U and only U will be facing the consequences of Ur actions and hopefully Ur actions will be leading to a Better U.

Robert Kiyosaki, of *Rich Dad, Poor Dad* fame, came up with this beautiful explanation which will make you think twice before making choices about Ur ultimate Career goal. Where do U want to end up being ??!! His explanation is outlined below:

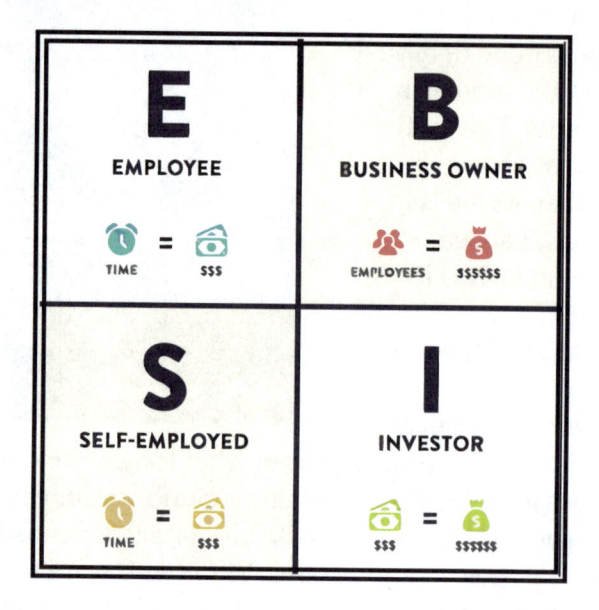

E EMPLOYEE TIME = $$$	**B** BUSINESS OWNER EMPLOYEES = $$$$$$
S SELF-EMPLOYED TIME = $$$	**I** INVESTOR $$$ = $$$$$$

An **Employee** is generally someone who works for another person or a company. This is the most common form of Career choice. Here U might be working for a person who is engaged in some form of Business – Small or Large, whether it is a Construction business or a Doctor's Office or any professional Organization, or working for the Government, or Serving the nation through Military or other Civil services.

Employees generally depend on their superiors for directives, and their future is pretty much in the hands of the Employer, whether it is a person, a Company, an Agency or the Government itself. If the Employer makes some bad decisions then the future of the Employee is at great risk. Employees usually exchange their Time for Money. Sometimes, depending on the Employment, they may be forced to put in MORE time for the same amount of Money. This is the **most disadvantageous** of the 4 Types being discussed here. The **ONLY bright side** to this is that, the amount of Responsibilities on Ur shoulder may be very little, depending on what level of employment U R engaged in.

Self-Employed people have mastered a trade or skill and sell their **Skill and/or Time** in exchange for money or other monetary resources. Self Employed will include people like Doctors, Lawyers, Accountants, Musician, Actors, Bakers, Consultants, Masseuse, Plumbers, Electricians or Masons just to name a few. All these folks have Specialized Skills that they Sell for a Living. Most small business owners are considered Self-Employed people because, unless they have systemized their small business to the point where it can run without their presence, all they have done is Created a Job for Themselves. And the worst part of this is they **work for the Worst Boss** there is – Themselves. U cannot take a break from the business unless it is systemized to run without U. If U R an Actor or a Performing Musician or a Surgeon, guess what, **nobody else can do Ur Job to make U the money**, so U need to reconsider and restructure Ur whole small business to the point that

Choices...

Choices...

Self-Employed is not going to become an overwhelming job whereby U R not only the CEO of Ur company but also the Chief Custodian.

A **Business Owner** is the person who created a system which generates money through the sale of some products or services which are in demand by a larger community of consumers. The Business Owners employ multiple layers of Employees who are delegated the tasks and responsibilities of the operation of the Business. Simply put, a **Business** in the service industry is usually an Entrepreneurial effort to solve a problem for another human at a **Profit**. Once that effort gets systemized, the Entrepreneur generally need not put their complete time and effort into the operations of the Business. However, if the delegated parties make any mistakes, the whole **cost of the mistake** is mostly borne by the Company or Business Owner alone. While the Business owner can enjoy the luxuries of free time because most of the laborious work has been delegated, the amount of responsibilities and quick decision making can become very demanding.

An **Investor** is usually just a spectator of the Show, a person who has done their homework thoroughly about the Business or Venture or Real Estate that they are planning to Invest in. An Investor's time is not directly equated to money. They always plan for Long-Term Returns. Their Effort is not spent making a living; instead their Time and Effort is spent finding ways to create more sources of Income Without Working – that is, in creating

360 Degrees of Life

Passive Income. They Do their Work initially and probably start as an Employee but very quickly move to the Self-Employed stage and soon move into the Investor stage. Start Investing in a very early stage of life. The sooner U can learn the skills of Investing, whether it is Ur Time or Money or Other Resources, the faster U will be on track to what is known as **Financial Freedom** – a situation where U have the **CHOICE** to do What U want to Do, When U want to Do it, and NOT depend on anyone else for funds and resources.

What U choose to Do or Become is entirely upon U and Ur choices. When the going gets tough, the tough ones fight for what they want to achieve. That is the most attractive and desirable trait in any human being. Nobody likes a quitter. Circumstances may make or break everyone. It can break the good people, the gentle ones, the brave ones and the weak ones; and those that it doesn't break, it can kill. There is no shame in being a broken person – broken by circumstances – what matters is the choice you make to pick up the pieces and start rebuilding. That requires a load of determination and the will to put time and effort where it is needed.

After we make mistakes there R only three things we can do: Admit the mistake, Learn from the mistake and Never repeat that mistake again. Everything that happens in this world has two sides to it: **What** happened and **How** it all happened. There is often a very fine line between this What and How, and this line is usually where the truth of the matter is hidden. When U Succeed in a Venture, look at what U did Right and **Repeat** it. If U fail in a Venture, look at what ALL U did Right and what one thing U did Not Do Right and then **Don't Repeat** it. A formula for success almost always includes **systematic** and **repeatable** processes producing the Desired Results.

Choices...

Once a kid asked his mentor, "What are clouds made up of?" The mentor, who was an IT professional, answered it from his paradigm and said, "Clouds are mostly made up of Linux servers." The answer was correct from his standpoint, but the kid looked at the mentor as though he was speaking a foreign language.

Here the question was pretty straightforward, but the mentor did not make an effort to understand the **context** of the question. Instead he answered the question from only his perspective. Sometimes the Choices U make are totally dependent on Ur viewpoint, so always keep in mind the people that are going to be affected by Ur **Choices**.

When U take on a Leadership role, Ur choices are going to affect those who are in Ur group. As a leader, if U only look at things from Ur viewpoint, then U pretty much risk Ur very own existence.

The Choices U make shud always be Ethical, then the only other thing U need to consider is whether that Choice is being made for the **benefit** of a greater group. Always put Urself in the other person's shoes when making a Choice on their behalf, especially if U are in a position of authority over the other person. If U R aware of the consequences of Ur Choices on the other person's Life and if U R **Mentally Awake** and **Morally Straight**, Ur Choices will always be Right for the larger group of individuals.

Ralph Waldo Emerson wisely quoted that, "To be yourself in a world that is constantly trying to make you something else is the greatest accomplishment." That message tells U not to lose Ur **Individuality**. It sure is a great accomplishment, because sometimes U wud have to go against a whole

82   360 Degrees of Life

society and its beliefs and viewpoints. Ur Individuality reflects Ur interests and beliefs. U are taught to Walk and Talk and Deal with others. But that does not mean U shud lose Ur identity. Every person is born different, with a Unique set of attributes. That **Uniqueness** is what makes us humans so special. Try to preserve that Uniqueness and blend it with the Skills U learn from Ur world. U don't have to **act different** just to be different. But if U R different in ways beyond Ur control, then Cherish that difference and use it as Ur Strength.

Don't do anything out of peer pressure or depression or any other external factor. Remember most **external factors** are temporary, so don't let them alter Ur inborn qualities. Whatever U Choose to Do in Life, do it for Enjoyment, Not to Impress anyone, Not to Deceive anyone. Whatever U Choose to make a Living at, Do it out of Passion and not Pressure. When U do anything with Passion and enjoy it, it no longer becomes just a Job. When U change Ur Outlook to Life in this way, suddenly U will see a whole world of Difference, and the results will be better as well. People who work at something because they have a passion for it are usually the ones that make a difference in their chosen field.

Choices...

When Everything around U seems to be going up against U, keep in mind what Henry Ford said, "When everything seems to be going against you, remember that the airplane takes off against the wind, not with it." This saying is in line with the above statement that Ur external factors should **Not** be the only things that affects Ur Choices. They may influence Ur **Choices** but they shud not decide them.

Finally it's not just the Destination that is important, U shud also make sure that U R taking the **Right Path** for Ur Journey. This comes back to the point that all the Choices U make should be Legal, Moral and Ethical. If more and more people follow that path, the World will definitely become a nicer place. This world is **Not Getting Bad** because we have more Bad people now, it is going Bad because the Good People are **Staying Silent** and also because Ethics and Morals are being tossed out from most teachings.

Here are my Choices with regards to Life...

Choices...

Choices...

360 Degrees of Life

Winning Attitudes and Habits

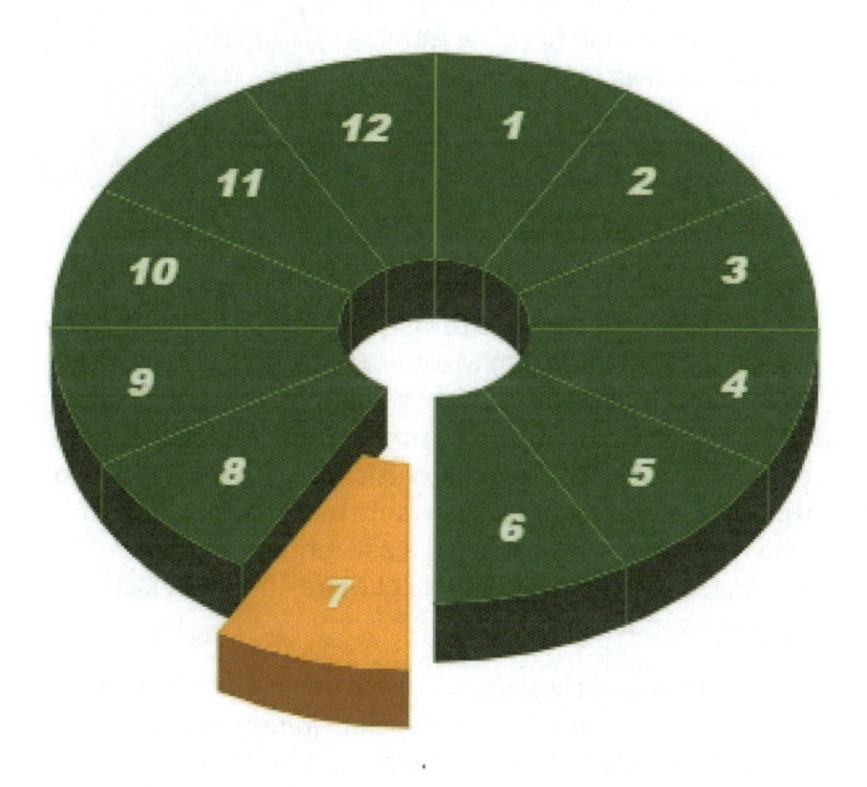

Winning Attitudes and Habits

They can Make U or Break U – Choose the Right kind.

The will to win is nothing without the willingness to **PREPARE** to win. Put a 100% effort in preparing to win, then Ur winning is assured. It is a very strong message, U can have all the Right tools and Right Aptitude to win in any endeavor, but before that U must have the Attitude and Willingness to Prepare to Win. U have to put the time and effort needed in the preparation to Win, and that is possible only through Attitude adjustments and positive Habit formations.

In the physical world or in the virtual gaming world, we ALL want to WIN. Nobody likes to lose, be it a game of scrabble with Ur mother or an arm wrestle with Ur buddy. In order for us to win in this Game of Life, we ought to have what some might call "**Winning Attitudes and Habits**." U will be picked on any team if U have the *right attitude*, even if U are a little weak on Ur skill sets. Nobody wants to deal with a person who has amazing skill sets but a bad attitude. Skills are always learnable, but it takes a Lot More effort to adjust someone's attitude.

Make it a **habit** of always telling the **truth**. It saves U so much time and energy, and U will appreciate it more and more as U get older and more involved with people in Ur society. U know Y it is so cool; If U tell the truth, U don't have to remember anything, as noted by Mark Twain. When U lie about something, U need to remember what U said first and then the next story and so forth. Lots of wasted energy, Bcos in the end, it is guaranteed that the truth will come to light anyway.

Our **Integrity** is determined by always doing the right thing, even when nobody's watching. By definition, Integrity is the **practice of being honest** and showing a consistent and uncompromising adherence to strong moral and ethical principles and values. It is a very **valuable habit** U can practice to maintain a good character base. A person of integrity is most certainly a dependable person in all circumstances.

How U see Ur **future** is very important because the way U see Ur future determines Ur **thinking**. Ur thinking Today determines Ur **performance** today, and Ur performance today determines the **actions** U take and the actions U take today determines where Ur life will lead U tomorrow – one step **closer to Ur dreams and goals** or one step farther away. So the vision U have about Ur future is very critical.

Consider a few legendary players from around the world. Most of U recognize football/ soccer legends like Pele, Lionel Messi and basketball legends like Michael Jordan. When U think about these team players, would U say they **played** for their teams or they performed for their teams? Undoubtedly U can say they **PERFORMED** for their teams, and that is what makes them more valuable than any of their personal stats. So in every team U ever become a part of, whether it is for sports or at Ur work, be a **Performer** and not just a Player. It is the

Performers that often lead the teams to victory.

U can rest assured that Ur **future** lies in Ur hands and depends mostly on how U perform in any given situation. When U start **taking responsibility** for Ur actions, Ur life starts changing for the better. This one step alone marks the beginning of Ur success track for life. The moment U realize that everything that happens to U depends on the choices U make now and the actions U take going forward, U feel **Empowered**. Ur life at any given moment is the result of all the choices U made up until that point.

We humans are NOT known for Accepting responsibility. Even the biblical stories from the days of Adam and Eve are proof of that. When God questioned Adam about the Forbidden Fruit, Adam did what most men have done ever since the beginning of time. Adam said "Lord, let me tell you about that woman YOU gave me; she made me... ." So, God asked Eve about the Forbidden Fruit, and Eve did what most people DO in our society today, she just passed it on and accused the snake. Historically speaking, this is how most of us humans have been dealing with accepting responsibility. If U start believing in **Accountable Actions** and start behaving based on that, U will see how Ur life starts changing for the good.

People tell U to plan for a rainy day or save for a rainy day. Make sure to have something to fall back on, have a backup plan etc. My question to U is, Y?? Y are U expecting failures and setbacks?? Yes, they are inevitable in some ways, but building Ur life strategies to overcome failures is not the right approach. Plan Ur life goals and build strategies so U don't fail, so U don't have to depend on that backup. Having a backup plan is always a smart idea, but putting Ur main attention on the backup plan is not. U don't have to believe in Zen masters to understand the basic concept that "whatever U focus on usually becomes Ur reality." So put Ur focus on the good stuff, good thoughts, good deeds and – before any of that – define "*good*" in Ur own terms. (see Chapter 4)

Take calculated risks in life, and if anything fails, fall forward like a long jumper. At Least you'll get to see what you're falling for. Planning for the future often includes planning for contingencies. That is what makes *planning* the first step to success. When V fail to plan, V R planning to fail. Nobody in their right mind plans to fail in anything they do, so planning is very important, just as important as **following through** on the plan. Every failed experiment brings you one step closer to Ur success, Yes!! I am sure you have heard that, but R U taking that risk to perform?? R U prepared to face that failed experiment, that is the real question here, Bcos unless U R prepared to face that and make that move, U R NOT ready to succeed. The Choice is Urs.

An **Attitude of Gratitude**, goes a Long way in life. A mere Thank You when delivered emphatically has more power than any material gifts you might offer to another human. Always **Say it, like you Mean it**. The first people to Thank in Ur life are Ur elders who taught U how to "talk the talk" and "walk the walk". It would mean a whole world to them to hear U say a whole-hearted **Thank You**.

Winning Attitudes and Habits

From the time U are born, U are indebted to numerous people, from the *midwife* or *nurse* that delivered U to the *elder* that encouraged U to take Ur first step, to the *teacher* who taught U how to read and write, to the *friend* who taught U how to throw a ball or ride a bicycle, to the *barista* who makes Ur morning coffee, to the *spouse* who takes care of U and Ur young one, to the *child* who takes care of U during U senior years, to the *doctor* who cares for Ur ailments, to the day the *undertaker* comes to Ur doorstep. For ALL the services U have received all thru Ur life, U have to **be thankful** to a lot of people along the way, some U remember profusely others U forget conveniently. Saying Thank You to others can be the foundation for the healthiest of all human emotions, **Gratitude**.

If U have **True desire** for anything good U want to achieve, it is proof to U that it is already Urs. When U have Ur heart in the right place, somehow things seem to come to Ur help. When U seek the right stuff whole-heartedly, it usually appears. Now don't think it to the extremes to disprove this fact. There is no use for that. Like Martin Luther King said, "The time is always **right** to do what is **right**." (emphasis mine).

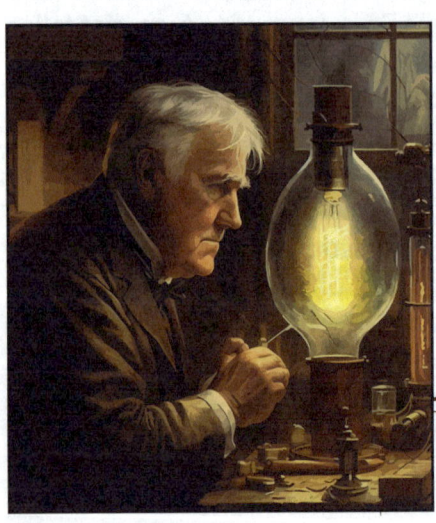

Thomas Edison is quoted as saying, "I have not failed 10,000 times—I've successfully found

10,000 ways that will not work." Edison almost proved one of the old adages: Where there is a will, there is always a way.

Anything **Good** U want in Life, U can HAVE, as long as U have the strong **desire** and **will** to go get it and U do not stop UNTIL U get it. Once U get what U want, reach back and help someone else get what they want to achieve and together everyone moves ahead. **Try to always form TEAMs around you**. One of the ways to look at what a TEAM is – Together Everyone Achieves More. There is no place for "I" in a Team. The sooner we identify that, the better off we will be in that Team.

U may ask, "Can't I become successful by myself??" The one word answer is YES. Yes, U can become successful all by Urself, but the levels of success U can achieve as a Team is Far More than anything U can achieve by Urself. Long ago humans figured out that they need the company of other humans for survival. Aristotle said, "Man is by nature a social animal; an individual who is unsocial naturally and not accidentally is either beneath our notice or more than human. Society is something that precedes the individual." In short – **Man cannot live alone**.

Modern humans are one of the most social species of all mammals. Our ever-evolving brains have developed to rely on our communal existence. Humans have developed distinctive languages to efficiently communicate as well. Our innate desire to stay connected with others has led to explosive innovations in the arena of gadgets, communication and the whole concept of electronic social media. As a couple of professors from the Bangor University in the UK once said, "Our inner ape craves company."

The days are gone when people tried to stay connected using pigeon mail, physical mails or telephones, the need to stay connected has generated a plethora of tools all because V don't want to live alone, V need company of other human beings. Tools like Facebook, Instagram or Discord or any of the social media apps are keeping people connected across the globe.

It is our responsibility to do the Right thing all the time, doing the Right thing usually means doing what is Legal, Moral and Ethical. It is a fact that at any given time, Everyone acts and does the best they can in the given situation – with the knowledge they have. Believe it, Everyone, including U, will **ALWAYS Do Ur Best** at any given moment. When dealing with other humans, Ur attitudes are as important as Ur behavior itself.

Despite our best efforts, V are all liable to make **mistakes**. Some of them might be trivial mistakes while some may be more serious or even fatal. When people make mistakes, it takes a certain level of maturity for others to forgive them and forget about it. If the person who made the mistake is making a sincere **apology** to U, **accept** it and move on with Ur life. Whether U maintain that relation or not is totally up to U. Sometimes, their mistakes might have hurt Ur feelings or Ur ego. But when U forgive that person, U **free up Ur mind** of a burden, the burden of anger, the burden of hatred, the burden of contempt.

Similarly, if U R the one who made the mistake, **Be Sincerely Sorry** for your act. Do whatever it takes to restore the other person's ego that U might have hurt unknowingly. If Ur actions caused heartache to the other person, make sincere apologies. Be **truly remorseful,** and if U value that relationship, vow to never repeat that mistake knowingly or unknowingly.

Create **Meaningful Relationships** around Urself. Relationships in terms of parent/ children, husband/ wife, partners, friends, siblings, employee/ employer and anything else U can come up with. Make it meaningful, make it **worthwhile**. U can have all the wealth and all the riches U want, but if U don't have people around U to enjoy any of that in a meaningful way, then it is all pretty insignificant. Several studies have shown that unless U R engaged in some sort of meaningful relationships and social interactions, Ur life will not be satisfying and a lot of Ur accumulated money will probably go to medical expenses or counseling and that sort of thing.

U will NEVER see self-centered, happy individuals. **Happy people** are often the ones that **contribute** more to society than they take from it. Try to **understand the needs** of others around U and see how you can help them at their times of need. Like Elon Musk professes, make positive net contributions to society. Give out More of what U can afford to Give and Take in Only what U need. U Really Cannot Take anything with U at the end, U know.

As different as we all are, we all need to Learn to **CoExist**. Any awe-inspiring picture is often best portrayed in color. To depict a beautiful object, artists will need more than 1 color to do any justice to their subject. In the same way, to make any worthwhile contributions to mankind, U will need to make an impact on more than one kind of person, and for that U will need to open up Ur minds and accept **Diversity**. Our world is So beautiful mainly because of its Diversity.

Diversity in any group improves its dynamics. It opens Ur mind to infinitely more possibilities in life which U had no idea before. We may all look different, but we all breathe the same oxygen, and we all bleed the same color blood. As Genetics suggests, diversity is important because it gives our species a better chance at survival. However, genetic diversity is usually lost when populations get isolated, which decreases the species' ability to adapt and survive.

As important as it is to embrace Diversity, so is the need to Look Right in any situation. Always **Dress for Success**… I'm sure somewhere along the way U have heard the saying, "You Are what you eat," simply meaning the composition of our body reflects the nutrients V put into them. In the same way, research has proven that the clothes V wear directly or indirectly affect our *attitude*, *mood* and *confidence*. If V change the way V dress, the way V feel automatically changes. When U dress up for a meeting, U R letting the other person know that U have respect for them – U respect the time the other person is spending for U. These are subtle ways of letting others know how U feel about that interaction.

It is a popularly held belief that Ur "looks" can influence the way others perceive and respond to U. Sadly, how U dress can sometimes be the **only reason** people approve or reject U. Some of the newer studies show that what U wear not only has an effect on the outside but also on the inside. When U feel good on the outside, U are more likely to feel good on the inside, meaning inside Ur mind, which in turn boosts Ur energy levels and self-confidence thus affecting Ur overall attitude and performance itself. When U are in a better mood, Ur interactions with others around U tend to be more encouraging and friendly, and U tend to be more productive too. Ultimately dressing Ur best for any occasion brings out the **Best Version of U**. Color, style, and material – all have psychological links and are often tied to memories. What U wear affects how U feel so much that it can even distort and determine Ur thoughts and judgments. **Dress for the occasion**. U need not over do it and most certainly **do not under do it**.

Winning Attitudes and Habits

Have U heard sayings like, **"Never ever Quit"**, and "U Lose Only when U Quit trying." ?? Those are attitudes to embrace, attitudes that helped the first person who created fire by rubbing rocks together and motivated the last person U saw succeed in a worthwhile endeavor. U gotta keep trying. Make it a point that Quitting is UnAcceptable unless what U R doing actually may harm U. Be determined that U will not Give Up. When U have made up Ur mind like that, then there is nothing in this world that can wear U out and Everything in this world will become achievable for U. This one mental attitude is enough to help U withstand the toughest of situations in life. The famous Entrepreneur **Jack Ma**, of Alibaba fame, said something like this, Today might be difficult, Tomorrow is going to be worse, but If U are determined NOT to give Up, then U will see that the day after tomorrow is **Beautiful** and totally worth it. And the sad reality like Jack says, most average people give up by tomorrow evening, figuratively speaking. If only they had the mental strength to hold on till the day after tomorrow...

Crawling is Acceptable,
Falling is Acceptable,
Crying is Acceptable,
Failing is Acceptable;
Quitting is NOT!

Everyone has talents and knowledge to succeed, but the question I have for U is, do U have the guts to FAIL?? How U look at that failure makes all the difference in the world. One way to look at it is **FAIL – First Attempt In Learning**. If U don't fail once in a while, U R probably not even trying anything worthwhile. It is very critical to understand that failure is just an event. Don't dwell on it. Learn from it, and keep moving towards Ur vision and purpose. It is not easy to fail at anything, Bcos, in order for U to fail, U must be brave enough to try something U have never done before. Now, that action needs some serious guts. People who have attained huge successes R usually people who have bravely crossed their comfort zone and tried something creative.

If someone brings to Ur attention a problem that they R facing, look at the bigger picture, look at Y it is a problem to that person. Is it just the person, or is it a problem faced by more than just that one individual?? If it is a more common problem, try to find the opportunity in it, to find a solution that can help more than just that person. Now U have an **entrepreneurial mindset**, that is an attitude U can embrace. About 70% of the population depends on the solutions provided by the other 30% that created it. So be the solution provider and not the problem creator.

Iron is an incredibly strong metal, but it is self-destructive when it rusts. Similarly, people destroy themselves thru their own negative mindset. To prevent the rust from ruining the iron, V apply paint or other anti-rusting coatings to it. The same way, to avoid self-destructive habits, V can strengthen our minds with positive and affirmative thoughts. Creating positive and self-affirming habits is a sure way to exceed Ur own expectations in all walks of life. One of the most self-destructive habits that humans practice is their Self-limiting beliefs. Humans are preconditioned by society in numerous ways to believe that U cannot do this, U cannot do that, and a long chain of "what if..." These R all nothing but **Guilt-based** and **Fear-based** false theories passed on from one human to another. U have to overcome this, and one of the effective ways is to have a solid self-motivator for Urself.

Research has shown that students with savings accounts in their own names R about 70% more likely to graduate from college. They feel motivated to graduate Bcos they feel a sense of power to control their future. So start a savings account when U or Ur kid enters their teenage years. It is a great way of getting into the Habit of Saving for the needs of tomorrow. Whether they decide to go to college or not is entirely up to them, but at least they will form a very **powerful habit** of managing their finances. No matter what they choose to do to earn a living, to advance to the next successful stages of life, **Managing their Money** will be a very desirable skill.

The right time to teach **anyone** about money management is **NOW**!! If U think otherwise, what do U think is a better time?? Human brains are so advanced – researchers have found out that we can teach calculus to a 4 year old because they can process that information efficiently. Kids are like sponges, they will soak up everything around them. If we expose them to the "*good*" stuff they will absorb the "*good*" stuff, whether it is good **habits** or good **morals** or good **sellable skills**. The KEY is then to introduce them to all that "GOOD" stuff as early as possible. And it is never too late to teach/ learn the good stuff. It helps U get to the so called "*good side*" of life. Like Aristotle said, V become what V repeatedly do. Anything V repeatedly do is often called a 'habit'; so if U choose to excel in everything U do, **excellence** will then become part of Ur habits.

Cultivating Good Habits shud be a Priority in Ur Life. The sooner U start, the better and easier it will become. Managing Time and Managing Money R the most challenging yet most satisfying of all learnable skills. The beauty of it is that, between Time and Money, U are covering everything in Life that we see humans running the rat race for. U see people run after time because it is so limited, and U always feel U R running out of it, which is True. People run after Money because no matter how much U have of it, many people feel they never have enough. So between those two, if U learn to strike a balance and get into the habit of managing both those resources, U will feel pretty well stabilized.

Good Habits to cultivate may include simple things like:

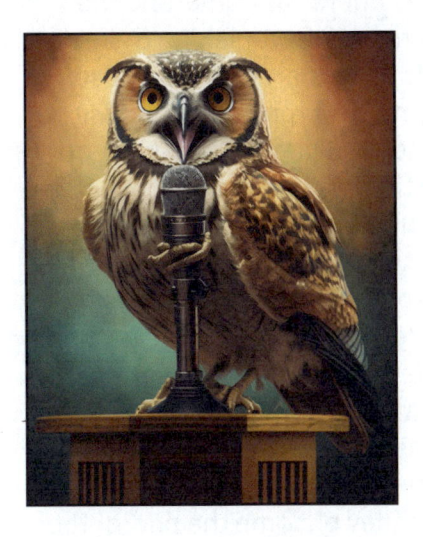

Being Honest

Being Punctual

Being Fit

Being Successful
(Yes!!! It can become a Habit – a good one that is)

Being Humble

Being Grateful

and so on … .

In society most people pass the responsibilities to others, which is one of the reasons we see bad behaviors in public places and in general. Good Habits and Good Manners have to be taught on what I call "home ground." This is anywhere that an individual is existing – any place where the individual is having a social interaction with another human being. No institution or organization shud be held responsible for it. Yes, the teacher's job is to teach the good stuff, but it is the duty of every individual around the children and youth to enforce that good behavior. We all tend to move away from someone who is engaging in unacceptable behavior. Y?? That is an **attitude adjustment** we need to bring about in today's society. If we see something wrong being done, as a responsible person we need to **step up and respond** to it in a sensible way. There's an old African proverb widely accepted in several cultures that is – ***It takes a village to raise a child***. It is not just the parents or the teachers that affects the child and their thinking. The whole environment around that child affects it.

It is a good idea to teach children to do chores at home, and the younger U start making them do little chores around the house, the more responsible they will be as adults. They don't have to do anything major. The idea of helping around the home plants the seeds in their mind that they are a **part** of something bigger. They feel valuable and when they are older, they will feel more useful in the groups they belong to, whether it is the family or a team. Make them feel like the most important link of the chain. The most important link in any chain – is the weak one, the smallest one, the one that gets the most attention. Make them understand the stronger they become the part of the chain the stronger the whole chain is.

If U develop a **habit** of doing small things – chores for Ur family, classroom, team, society – U will become a better person. U will be more likable, desirable and **valuable** for any team, organization or community. U have to learn to lead on Ur own; the sooner U can learn this skill the better. Taking the initiative to do the right thing, or to do what the situation demands without someone else asking U to do it, is a very desirable skill in any individual. The people who show this kind of initiative are often categorized as **natural leaders**.

These are the individuals who create the waves and have the crowds follow them. In any given crowd of people, about 95% of the people there, R followers and U can spot the other 5% by simply observing their behaviors with others. Effective

Leadership is a Skill, meaning, it is **Learnable**. Once U learn to lead on Ur own, U start creating visions for Ur chosen path, and that is the beginning of Ur own success story. So develop the **habit** of leading on Ur own, being self-motivated. When U develop Urself to the level where U R serving other people, U R elevating Urself to a whole new level. U R not just successful. U R significant.

When U start taking Ur own path, U R bound to make mistakes and that is OK. Remember, every mistake U make adds to Ur experience level, and with increased experience U eventually reduce Ur mistakes. So, everytime U make a mistake U might say U R getting closer to perfecting the task. Ralph Waldo Emerson has contributed some very meaningful insights about this, like, "Do not go where the path may lead, go instead where there is no path and leave a trail." And "Our greatest glory is not in never failing, but in rising up every time we fail."

In life there are very few things that we learn perfectly the first time we attempt to. The first time we learned to walk, we must have fallen down a 1000 times, but every time we jumped right back up and tried to walk again until it became a natural act. Similarly, we learn most things in life by correcting our mistakes and adjusting our attitudes. Every time V fail, V must rise again and try again with more focus. The rising up again is the most important part. It shows Ur attitude towards succeeding in the task at hand.

Life is not always fair, in Ur definition of fairness. **Accept this** and move on. Life can get crazy busy and U might face failures at times too, but none of that should scare U. How well U handle these situations determines Ur abilities and Ur innate personality. Remember to perform at Ur very Best at the darkest hours of Ur life. That is the time when U have to put all Ur skills and tactics and knowledge to work, and still follow Ur heart and Ur intuition. Because there is always a Bright side on the other side of darkness, nothing is permanent. Brightness usually follows darkness. After a Hurricane comes a peaceful Rainbow. If U dwell on Ur problems and decide not to move, U R not facing a problem, but a 'poor choice'.

If U draw Ur courage from a 1,000 people standing behind U, then U are a **Leader**, but if a 1,000 people draw their courage because U R **Leading** them, then U know U have become an **Effective Leader**. If U feel confident in Ur decisions bcos U have a strong team, then U can treat Urself as a good leader because U need to be a good leader to lead a strong team. But if Ur Team feels confident because YOU are leading them, then together U and Ur team can make some great contributions in Ur field of choice.

Like they say, if U wish to be the King of the jungle, it is not enough to act like a king, instead U must Become the King, by All means necessary that are Legal, Moral and Ethical. Believing in Urself and Ur strengths is a **must** for an effective leader, but so is believing in Ur team and their strengths. That way, together U and Ur team can achieve Ur visions. So make sure U put Ur Faith in the right place. Nobody will remember All the times U were Right, but Everybody will remember when U were wrong. It's just human nature. **Don't let the Others** set expectations for U, coz then U might be starting very low and U might stay there. U might be capable of Much More than what others know and think about U. Maybe U have not matured enough to let others know of Ur strengths. So **Believe in Urself and Ur Strengths** and move ahead towards Ur Vision for the future.

Social Respect and Acceptance

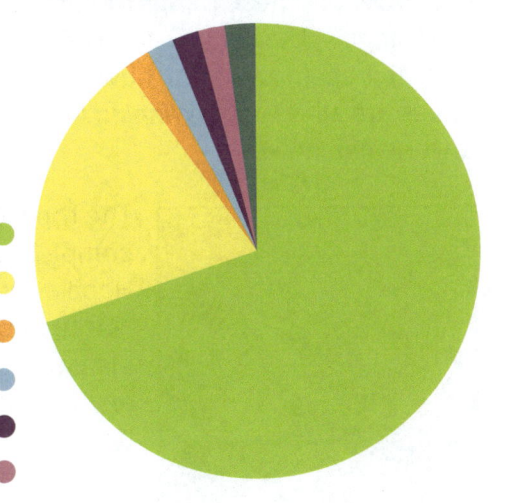

- Ur Manners/Ethics 🟢
- Ur Values 🟡
- U Money 🟠
- Ur Beauty 🔵
- Ur Power 🟣
- Ur Skills 🌸
- Ur Intelligence 🟢

As U can see, if U take a 360° look at Ur Life and see how different things affect the Acceptance and Respect U get in society, U will clearly see that 70% of it depends on Ur Manners/ Ethics. Basically How U treat others and How U deal with others around U. Ur Skills, Ur Money and all those other things contribute to less than 3%, and yet somehow people tend to give those things a lot of importance. U need to keep the focus on the Main things. Ur Ethics and Values have FAR more importance than anything else in Life. Look at the list of a **Dozen things** and think, "What is So special about these things??"

★ Being On Time
★ Being Energetic
★ Being Dependable
★ Being Honest
★ Being Coachable
★ Being Cheerful
★ Being Helpful
★ Being Prepared
★ Being ready to go that extra mile
★ Presenting Good Body language
★ Being passionate about UR work
★ Having a Good Work Ethic

Winning Attitudes and Habits

Winning Attitudes and Habits

If you look in depth at each of the items in this list you will see, NONE of these things requires any Talent. To do any of the things in the list you need **ZERO Talent**. That being said, look at it again and think how important each of them is. These are all 🗝 **Winning Attitudes and Habits** that anyone can have.

The topic of **Habits** is never complete without a discussion of Hobbies, and U shud have Hobbies, Not to impress anyone but to please Urself. A Hobby can be anything from collecting different types of dead leaves to traveling, to photography, to coin collections, you name it. V humans are very diverse, and so are our hobbies. Like that proverb, *One man's trash is another man's treasure*, so a candy wrapper is a trash for someone, while for a person who collects candy wrappers from around the world it's a collectible item. Develop Hobbies that will help U in Ur overall Vision for Life.

If U can adjust Ur attitudes and develop Sellable Skills out of something U love to do anyway, like a Hobby, then U can say U have a pretty good balance in Ur Life. So pick Hobbies that will help U at least in Each one of these areas :

One to Make Money
 – a **Career**

One to Keep you in Shape
 – something **Health** related

One to Jog Ur **Creative** Mind

One to Build Ur **Knowledge**

One to Grow Ur **Mindset**

360 Degrees of Life

Similarly, Our **Life** and **Style** will usually reflect who V R surrounded by, so make sure to stay close to the Inspired, the Motivated, the Open-Minded, the Passionate and the Grateful ones. Bcos these R the Winning Attitudes U can develop in order to reach Ur Success and Ur Happiness. The Inspired ones R always looking at the bright side of the story, they will be an encouragement to U while the Open-Minded ones will be there to help U think outside the Box, and U know a lot of times when V face a difficult situation, all it takes to resolve it is to simply think outside the box. The Passionate ones will be the one who shares, the same drive as U towards Ur final vision, and they will provide U that push when U feel weak.

U have to learn to Focus on the things U have the control over. Those R the things U can change, adjust and manipulate so that they all work together in favor of U and Ur vision. Many times, people are SO engrossed in things U cannot control like inflation or decisions by certain government officials, or the global market tumble or the weather. Yes, they are ALL important, and they ALL contribute to and Affect Ur life directly, but my question to U is, "How does getting upset help ?????" There is not much use in being upset about the inflation for example; what U can DO is make-grass root level changes in Ur habits and attitudes and make a positive impact in Ur immediate surroundings in a way that creates a ripple effect and possibly makes a positive impact on Ur society. Rather than complaining about things U cannot change, identify the things that U CAN change and make the Change U wish to See for the betterment of all. That is an Awesome attitude to have rather than sitting and complaining and dragging everyone down.

Things yoU can Control:

- Ur Actions
- Ur Attitude
- Ur Habits

Winning Attitudes and Habits

The Power U have over Urself is what makes the biggest impact in Ur Life. If U R a leader then it is Ur responsibility to make sure Ur Team understands what they control. This will in turn help them do their job well. If U have good habits that U showcase through Ur actions, then everyone around U or on Ur team will follow that. But if U set a bad example as a leader, this will produce undesired results.

V often attract things that V believe in; it's just nature's way of dealing with beings. If V carry a positive vibe around us, V tend to attract positive situations. It is like tuning into a radio station. If U want to listen to Jazz music, U have to be tuned into the Jazz radio channel and not the Country music channel. In a similar way, if U want to attract things U wish to have in Ur life, then **U have to be tuned into the energy** U want to manifest in Ur life. These are life choices U make that can build or break Ur future and Ur vision:

★ Learn to Listen before U Speak.
★ Learn to Earn before U Spend.
★ Learn to Understand before U Write.
★ Learn to Try Again before U Quit.
★ Learn to Maintain Relations B-4 U Make new ones.
★ Learn to Live Fully before U Die… .

When U become a person that can handle Urself under ANY circumstances in a calm and composed way, then U know U have matured and reached a whole new level of Success and Happiness. This happens only when U have a clear and concise mental picture of Ur Vision of Success and Happiness.

360 Degrees of Life

No matter Ur Age or Circumstances, there is always room to grow and improve Urself. Remember to have So much Pride and Healthy Self-confidence that U should be able to say confidently, "Do this if U want to end up like me..." Cultivate the **Habit of Being Consistent**, meaning Ur behavior has to be compatible with Ur Words and Ur Actions. U cannot act self-contradictory or hypocritically. If U claim in Ur words that U R a dependable person, then U shud be the first one to step forward when someone needs help.

If U are a person of Integrity, others shud be able to say with confidence that U will do the Right Thing, even when no one is supervising U. U don't have to be an avtar of Pistis to prove U R trustworthy, but U certainly have to demonstrate Ur qualities thru Ur actions. Being **Consistent** is a very desirable attribute for someone in any leadership position or for Life in general. If people can trust U, this speaks a LOT about **Ur Character**. A person of Integrity and moral Consistency will always be trusted and admired under any circumstance.

Everyone makes mistakes and faces failures in their journey through life. Making mistakes is not a crime; people who make mistakes are often the ones who **Dared** enough to Try something different from the norm. They are usually the ones who achieve a high-degree of success too, only because they were brave enough to take that most difficult step in the unknown direction – the **First Step**. Some see these failures as burdens for Life, while Others use them as Stepping Stones on a Learning Curve. That Attitude adjustment makes a world of difference. If U carry Ur mistakes as a burden on Ur journey they will Slow U down and Not let U think clearly. U have to step out of the situation and USE the **Lessons** from Ur failed attempts as stepping stones towards Ur goals.

Every mistake U make on a journey towards Ur vision is a valuable lesson learned, a lesson that can be passed on to others following Ur lead. The smart ones following Ur lead will learn from Ur mistakes and save time and energy, while the others... Smart and Intelligent followers will always attempt repeatable successful patterns and progress towards their goals and avoid making the same mistakes. I came across a beautiful depiction of this idea on some social media platforms via @successpictures as shown here.

If U R not willing to Learn New things, to Dare to attempt to take that First Step or to Learn from Ur mistakes, then No one can possibly help U. But if U shift gears and become **Determined to Learn** – Either New things or Lessons from Ur mistakes, then U become **UnStoppable** in Every endeavor U take.

When U R doing any task in Life, make an **Honest Effort** – Do Ur Best. Put Ur effort towards Ur goals until Ur last breath because whether U reach Ur Destination or U gain some Learning Experience along the way, they both are **Priceless**. Whatever be the end result, when U do Ur Best U have the **mental satisfaction** that U gave it Ur Best shot. Yes, Results are Important. But more important is the fact that U Tried and gave it Ur BEST shot. Always remember that **Fear** is an

Obstacle, and Obstacles are what U see when U take Ur eyes off Ur Goals. **Failure** is usually a Detour teaching U lessons along the way, and **Pain** is usually temporary, building U stronger. It is the **Determination to Continue** Despite of Fear, Failure or Pain that REALLY counts.

Ur **Attitude** to Face whatever comes Ur way with a Smile and Ur Hopes for a Better Future Shud be Bigger than Ur fears and worries. Knowing and understanding other people requires intelligence; knowing and understanding Urself defines true wisdom. Mastery over others can often be construed as strength, while **True Power** is in mastering Urself. It is not just what Others think about U that matters. What Truly matters is how U view Urself. Because **Ur view of Ur "Self"** will determine how U behave, and how U act and behave will determine Ur results. Being Truthful and having Integrity can be painful at times, but like a surgery, it has long-term positive results : whereas Lies and Shortcuts are like pain medication; it will give U temporary relief for sure, but it will have long-standing side effects and a negative impact overall.

Any **Challenge** U face shud be treated as an opportunity to learn a Life Lesson. Don't let them break U; instead use them to make a Stronger Version of U. Like that popular saying, What doesn't kill U, makes U stronger. As U work thru Challenges and work on making a better version of U, realize that U R making a more Confident version of Urself too. **Confidence** is not thinking U R better than anyone else, it is the realization that U have NO Reason to compare Urself to anyone else.

U can learn a Lot from any given situation if U just adjust Ur attitude toward it. Anything that U have to deal with that is annoying U is basically teaching U **patience**. If someone Abandons U, U can learn how to **stand up on Ur own**. Something that makes U Angry is teaching U **Forgiveness** and **Compassion**. Anything U fear is teaching U to be **Brave** and have the Courage to Overcome Ur Fear. Likewise, anything U cannot control is teaching U a valuable lesson to **Let Things Go**. Worrying over things like weather or aging are classic examples where people waste their energy. When U understand that there is no use getting upset about the rain, instead have the attitude adjustment and go grab that umbrella or rain jacket. Life will become easier by accepting things this way.

The difference between Crying and Trying is only ONE letter in spelling but a LOT of difference in meaning. **Crying** is sometimes considered a sign of weakness in some cultures while in reality it shud be considered as the easiest emotional release process. It is OK to Cry. We are all born Crying, and People who love U and care for U will Cry when U depart them from this world too, so whoever says that Crying anytime in between those phases of Ur life is not cool needs to re-evaluate their viewpoint. Some people are brave enough to cry in public, and others are more private in that emotional release process. Either way, understand that it is perfectly OK to Cry.

Trying is basically a state of mind that U go through when U don't want to Quit or don't want to give up on a task. U R also Trying, when U R getting Ur feet wet, when U R taking risks and making decisions and Choices. Trying does not apply to all facets of Life. U cannot TRY to be Truthful. U R Either Turthful or Ur Not. Trying describes Ur efforts at performing a difficult task or accomplishing something new or challenging.

To have the Confidence to stand behind Ur Decisions and the Courage to stand by its consequences is definitely a Winning Attitude to have. When U show the courage to face the consequences, U demonstrate true leadership in action. Decision-making itself is a challenge for several people, but it is a bigger challenge to own up to the consequences of that decision. It is the purest form of Accountable Action, because only a responsible person will have the Courage to stand by the consequences of their decisions whether the results are good or not.

Winning Attitudes and Habits

Winning Attitudes and Habits

These are MY winning Attitudes and Habits...

Sellable Skills 4 Ur Life

Sellable Skills 4 Ur Life
You may have skills, but are they SELLABLE ??

A Skill is the ability to do something well, based on Ur acquired knowledge.

Everyone has SOME skills. The real question is, Are they Sellable Skills?? If not, they R just for amusement. But nobody cares about them unless U can make a living with them. In other words, it's nice that you can spin a basketball on your pinky for 2 minutes or you can make a cherry stem knot with your tongue, but U shud **seriously** train Urself to do something that can earn U a decent living too.

When U enter **Ur Teen years**, each relative U run into, every coach U deal with, every new adult U interact with always seems to come at U with some great and marvelous idea on how **U SHUD** spend Ur life. What NONE of them might have told U is that how U choose to live Ur life is Ur Own Decision to make. Lot of times people suggest and throw ideas at the Youth, things **they wish** they had pursued or **they know** they did well with.

Very rarely will U come across someone who would admit that they tried this great idea but it failed and maybe U can try it slightly differently and make it happen. As rare as it can be, If U do come across someone like that, cling on to them because they are going to be the BEST Mentors U can find. A mentor who will steer U clear from the mistakes they have already made to save U time and energy.

360 Degrees of Life

Find Urself someone who will tell U the facts "as it is," whether U like it or Not. I am not talking about a News anchor or a talk show host either. I'm talking about someone U can look up to when U need guidance. Someone who can share facts without involving emotions. There is a reason why U R asked to describe Ur Role model right from Ur childhood days.

People who care for U and Ur well-being will be seen to question U about this Role model on several occasions. Usually U pick a Role model as someone who possesses most of the characteristics and values that U wish to have. **It is OK to have** multiple Role models, for different facets of life. U might really look up to someone when it comes to Career choices while their family life might be a mess. U might look up to a different individual when it comes to upholding Ethics and Morals. No one is perfect in every aspect, but on the same note, Everyone has Something Good about them. When U can identify that Good in the person and honor and respect them for that Goodness, U become more human and more likable.

U are the best judge of Urself because only U know Ur strengths, Ur weakness, Ur interests and Ur visions. That gives U the **power to choose** how U want to earn a living. Keep in mind the Power of knowledge and experiences too. Education is that tool that will enable you to take the steps towards Ur Vision. Education without Experience is like an engine without fuel, pretty useless. U may have all the Education in the world, but if U don't know how to put it to use, what good is it??

Sellable Skills 4 Ur Life

Look at how Ur life can be split up into 4 simple stages:

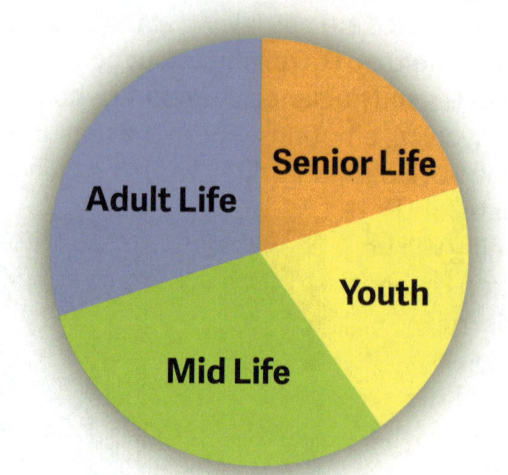

The first 20% of life, I call it the **Youth** phase. Basically U R carefree, U feel as though U are pretty much invincible, indestructible etc. U don't have a care in the world. This is also the phase where U have the **best opportunity** to learn and accumulate as many **life skills** as U can. When U R a youth, usually U do not have the responsibilities of earning a living, raising a family or finding a safe shelter. As a youth, most of Ur knowledge comes through formal Education. This is the stage when U learn the ABCs of life so to speak. What U learn here oftentimes helps U in the next stages of Ur life. I am NOT saying that learning calculus or history alone in school will help U lead a happy and successful life, but U need to know them in order to be **PREPARED** for whatever comes in the next stages of life as you move towards Ur dreams and goals. To climb any ladder U Have to start at the bottom rung.

118   **360 Degrees of Life**

As a **Youth**, U also have the privilege of trying to learn new lifeskills **without the pressure of time**, because U generally don't have to worry how Ur next meal is taken care of. So U just need to **Focus** on what U R learning and **learn it well** so in the future U can apply it to Ur chosen fields of work. U can **make money at anything** U so desire, all that varies will be the quality of lifestyle that U can afford with the chosen field of work. I am not talking about **personal satisfaction** level, just the quality of lifestyle. Every kind of work has its own **dignity of labor**. In any company the cleaning staff may be as important as the CEO, but the cleaners do not carry as much responsibility. Remember, the higher U climb a career ladder, the more people depend on Ur Choices and Ur Abilities.

The next 30% of life I call **Midlife**. This is the phase of life where everything starts to get more structured and more goal oriented. This is where **Career** takes the most predominance in most people's lives. This is the phase where people begin to settle down, make **major commitments** in life like buying a house, getting together in long-term meaningful relationships, raising children, working on improving Ur quality of life, and so forth. This is the phase of life where U have to become so **career focused** that U shud not have time to waste. These R the Most productive years of Ur career. This is the time U can take the most **aggressive risks**, because even if U make a bad decision, U have time to bounce back and keep moving towards Ur future Vision.

This is the phase of life when it is perfect to start getting involved in long-term investments and passive income structures. This phase of life is the most important **Planning Phase** of Ur life. What U do in this phase of life determines how well Ur retirement years will be. Ur **long-term investments** shud be aimed at supporting the bigger expenses U have to deal with in Ur Adult Life, the next phase of life, when U will be supporting Ur children and their ambitions too. Ur **passive income structures** shud be designed to provide the same quality of life when U R no longer able to work or when U R no longer generating a working income. Keep in mind there is always inflation affecting Ur cost of Living.

Ur **Midlife** is the most vital phase of Ur life in terms of **planning** and **preparing for the final stages of Ur Life**. How well U plan and prepare in this stage will determine how comfortably U can live during the next phases of Ur life. This is Ur **peak productivity** stage of life. Every action U take shud ultimately lead U in the direction of Ur vision for future. Like a sailboat, no matter how much it sways from side to side, it always moves in the general direction towards the destination. Ur **passive income structures** shud B able to produce income Without U working for it. They shud produce enough to enable U to live the lifestyle U desire without having to work or depend on someone else for money. Use Ur time to learn about Money management and investments. Earning a bunch of money and saving it for future use will not cut it. Ur money shud be making money for U while U R not looking at it, whether it is thru investments or thru business structures. That is the basis of Passive income structures.

The next 30% of Ur life I call it the **Adult** life. I call it the Adult phase Bcos this is the phase where U cannot afford to make mistakes, Bcos by now the number of people that depend on Ur decisions have gone up significantly. Career-wise U might have reached positions of **added responsibility** Bcos U now have not just the knowledge and skillset, but invaluable

Experience to support Ur knowledge too. U have learned most of the tricks of the trade and have learned and dealt with most of the problems that can possibly happen along the lines of Ur work as well.

This is the phase where U will be the ***role model*** for Ur next generation, whether it is at home to Ur own children or out in the community through value-based youth development organizations such as ***Scouting*** program. This is the time when U can devote Ur time and skills to ***Enable the future generations*** to make ethical and moral choices over their lifetimes. This will be the time U can teach the Youth the significance of the values of loyalty, integrity, courteousness, obedience, kindness, prudence, reverence and so on. This will be a phase where U make moral choices that can produce a positive impact in Ur society, whether it is in a small grassroots level or in a larger way. Ur impact depends on Ur abilities and Ur breadth of knowledge. Always remember, if U can positively influence one other person during Ur lifespan, Ur Life becomes 1 bit more worthy in the grand scheme of things. It is never just about U, but it is about what U can do for others that matters.

In the ***Adult phase*** of life, U shud put more focus into Ur future in terms of investment strategies and creating multiple sources of passive income. If U have not already done so, it's ***never too late***. Remember it is always the right time to do the right thing. Better late than never. U have to focus on how U can maintain Ur same quality of life without working and with the added expenses of healthcare as U advance in age. This requires a lot of serious planning. There are several resources U can resort to for retirement planning.

This is also the time U are beginning to invest into Ur children's dreams and visions. This is the time when U get to teach them Life Skills. This will be the time when U expose them to the beautiful, Life-changing concepts of **Time Management** and **Money Management**. Remember, youth always like to Model what they see. U can talk all U want, but unless U can demonstrate to them how it is done, they R not gonna follow U. So first get Ur ducks in a row and then teach them how it is done. U can educate Ur future generations on how to handle finances, and U can model how to plan for passive income generation. These are concepts that can be taught to very young children.

The fourth and final 20% of life, I call the **Senior** life. This is the stage of life where U get to enjoy the fruits of Ur labor through life. If U planned it well, U shud have multiple streams of passive income coming in to support the lifestyle U desire. U shud have investment strategies to support any healthcare demands that may arise or any family emergencies Ur next generations might have.

This shud be a time for U to relax with Ur loved ones. This is the phase where Ur life Goals have been achieved and U are living Ur dreams and visions.

Through every Phase of Life mentioned above, U will notice there are a Lot of Skills being talked about. Skills like Managing Money and Planning for the unexpected. These are all Learnable things too. There is always a time and place for Learning everything, so make sure U learn the Right things at the Right Time to avoid unexpected results. In case U missed out learning something in Ur younger years. Don't worry, the

360 Degrees of Life

Good News is that it is never too late to learn a New Skill. While U may not be able to learn to do acrobatics at age 65, U can achieve most reasonable goals.

A **Sellable skill** is anything U can exchange in return for something worthwhile. Most people may not agree, but **Selling** was one of the first professions of mankind. No matter how U want to look at it, everyone is selling something or the other to make a living. Some are selling **Products** while others are selling their **Skills**, some are selling their **Knowledge** and still others are selling their **Time**.

To choose a livelihood U have to decide what U want to sell to **other people** that can be of value to them. Remember U can only make a livelihood by selling to other people, because nothing else is going to give you the much needed money for Ur needs. Barter system still prevails in some parts of the world but mostly the economy runs with some form of money – physical or digital. **Money** is NOT the most important thing U might say. But it is pretty close to oxygen, I would say, because when U need it, **U Really do need it** – sometimes even to buy the Oxygen in the tank.

If U want to **produce** something and sell that product, U can be a Farmer, Fisherman, Graphic designer, Wordsmith, Programmer, Craftsman etc. In all these cases U will be using Ur knowledge gained through formal education or experience to produce things that are of interest to people who are willing to pay a **price for that product**. This is one of the first ways that people made a living; they produced something that they swapped or bartered for something else.

Sellable Skills 4 Ur Life

Then there is the selling of Ur **Skills**. People who do this exchange their specialized knowledge and associated skills for money. This would include Doctors, Nurses, Lawyers, Accountants, Engineers, Architects, Teachers, Coaches, Electricians, Plumbers, Masons and a whole plethora of other professionals. These are people who have learned specialized skills that they can use to solve other people's needs.

Then there is the selling of Ur **Time** in exchange for money. This includes people who use their basic life skills to make a living. They are not paid for their specialized skill set, but for the time they dedicate to their work. What U put in this category depends on Ur viewpoint on the significance of different jobs. A baby sitter, or a pet sitter can fall into this category and so does a security guard at the bank.

No matter what U choose to sell to make a living, make sure it is **worthwhile to Other**s and **Satisfactory to Urself**. For most of U, a third of Ur life will be spent in making a living, so U might as well choose a career U enjoy. And if U can make a living doing what U love to do anyway, there is no better way to **define Ur Success** in life. If U R passionate about driving, then being an Uber or Lyft driver might be a successful career track for U. If U love to play in water, be a lifeguard, if U would rather deal with fire, be a fireman. Go with what Ur heart desires. Believe it, U can make a living at it, U will find a way, U can do it.

124 360 Degrees of Life

Negotiation is a very important skill to learn in life. Some people say that U get what U deserve. That may be true in some instances, but most often than not **U get what U negotiate for**. People associate a lot of negativity with the word negotiation which is pretty sad. To Negotiate is to engage in a transaction where all people involved are satisfied at the end of the transaction. Nowhere has it been mentioned, except in sports, that in order for one to win the other has to lose. That is a misconception people live by, and for sure it causes a lot of mental agony. The 🗝 to any good or effective negotiation is to make both parties feel it is a **win-win** situation. Negotiate in a way that U are not hurting the other person involved financially or emotionally. There is plenty of quality Coaching available for effective negotiations. Learn some. They will be useful all throughout Ur life.

Do U know how to write a Check?? U can argue all day, that no one today **writes a check**. Yet, what U receive from Ur first job will still be called a **PayCHECK**. Who knows, someday U might be writing someone else's PayCHECK. So learn to write one. It is a very useful thing to know.

At the time this book was written, only a handful of countries make 50% or more of their transactions electronically. So learn how to deal with Cash and learn how to write Checks. U never know where Ur career might take U. There are still several places in the world where business transactions are based on physical, monetary exchanges – in simple terms – coins and currency.

One Awesome way to **accumulate a Lot of Skills** in Life is to use the Voice of Experience – meaning to learn from Others.

Use others's experience as Ur guidebook. U can learn from Other people's Successes and Failures as well. Learn and motivate Urself from Other people's successes and define and create Ur own paths while avoiding the mistakes that others have made. The Smart person learns from others' mistakes and avoids them. U can follow the simple and repeatable success formulas of others. Just model Urself on people who have skills similar to Urs, add Ur own special twist, and create Ur own Successful Life story.

If U fail in any task or any situation, remember Ur failure is not a sign of Ur **Character**, nor is it a sign of Ur weakness. Ur Character will be determined by How Fast U **bounce back UP**, not how many times U fall down. How many times U R willing to get back UP determines how far Ahead U will get in the Journey of Life. This was advice I received from my father when I faced what at the time I felt was a failure in my life. Like that poem from Kipling, Success and Failure are two imposters. Neither has any meaning except for the meaning U give it.

If U Choose to make a living by **monetizing on Ur hobby**, make sure that U are darn good at it and that U thoroughly enjoy it. Usually there is a gap between theory and practicality, and it is normally referred to as **REALITY**. While Ur hobby might be to paint rocks, and it might seem like lots of people are buying painted rocks at the "painted rocks" section at the local Hobby store, when U put it into perspective U need to face the reality of how

360 Degrees of Life

many people actually buy painted rocks. Will that be enough to support Ur needs?? There are no good or bad hobbies, any Skill that U put to use for personal pleasure can be termed a hobby. But to turn a hobby into a livelihood may not be practical.

Remember there R No Rights and there R No Wrongs. It all depends on how U look at things and the meaning U give to them. If Ur hobby involves creating something that might add value to someone's life or provide a solution for someone's problem then it is **Sellable**, and then U know U can monetize Ur Hobby. Hobbies like, photography, portrait painting, Artisan jewelry making, Cooking etc. can produce things that might interest other people. How much money U can make will depend on how much U R willing to put into it in terms of time and effort. While painting a rock for fun may not help U make a living, painting a rock sculpture in a commercial building might pay U a fortune. Choose wisely and Have fun.

Sellable Skills 4 Ur Life

These are MY Sellable Skills...

What U do with What U Have ???

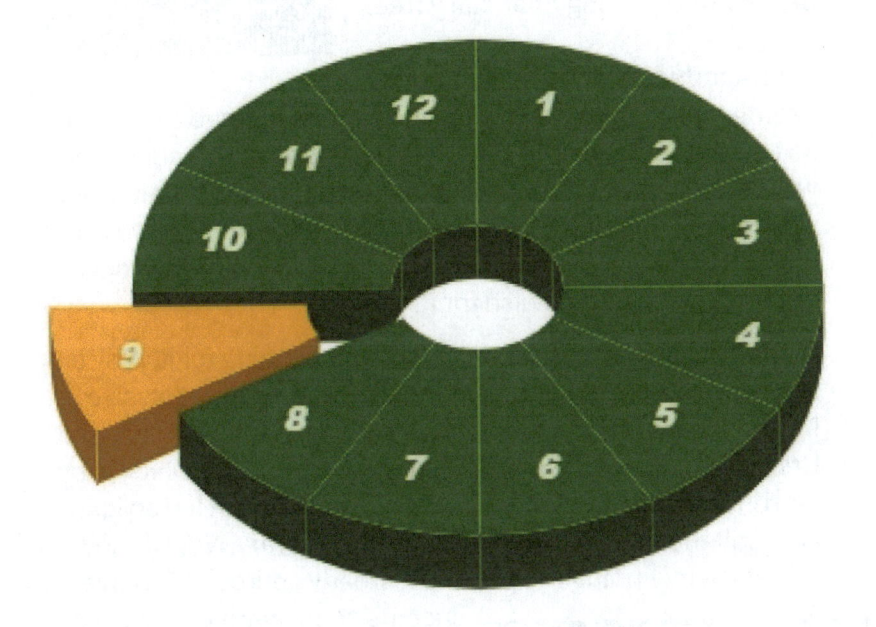

What U do with What U Have ???
This is FAR more important than How much U have.

It is nice to Earn a great deal of money, but What U do with what U earn is WAY more important in the game of life. U can have a huge earned income, but U have to manage Ur money well to become financially free. A concept that may be new to U – being financially free.

Financially free does NOT mean having millions and zillions, all it means is to have a CHOICE as to what U do with Ur time. It is a freedom to be able to do whatever it is that makes U Happy with Ur time at hand. One way to look at being Financially Free is to be able to live the lifestyle U desire without having to work for Ur money or depending on anyone else for it.

Money U can earn consistently, Without working for it, is often termed as PASSIVE Income. When U have enough Passive Income to support the lifestyle U wish to live, then U can put Urself in the category of Financially Free and Rich, which is by far the Best way of being Rich. People who win a lottery can also call themselves rich, but that's temporary. Now if they invest their winnings to provide a steady source of Passive Income, then they are on the right track. It is nice to receive a lot of money, through inheritance or other legit means, but if U don't use it wisely, U will soon lose it.

Remember U cannot take a *moving truck behind a hearse*, meaning U cannot take anything with U when U leave this world physically. History tells us that the powerful Egyptians and Mughals tried it, and all they got was robbed. Some believe The *Pyramids* were built in an effort to take the best of this world to the afterlife, and the story goes on. So since you R gonna leave it all behind any way, why fight to accumulate?? Live life with a purpose, to leave a **Legacy**. Ben Franklin said something like: If you don't want to be forgotten as soon as you are dead, either write something worth reading or do something worth writing. Leaving a legacy through Ur work means doing something for the betterment of the world, something worth writing about.

Everyone is rich in something. Some have plenty of money, some have plenty of patience, some have an abundance of knowledge, some have mere material possessions, some have a heart full of love, some have the valuable **Time** for others. Whatever it is, what U do with what U have makes a whole world of difference. If U use Ur resources wisely, U can not only improve Ur own lifestyle but also the lifestyle of those dependent on U, and perhaps, one step further, U can do something for the betterment of Ur Society as a whole.

Wealthy people are often not that much smarter than average people. They just have better time and money management habits. The keyword here is **habits**. I learned a very simple money management method which I profess to be so simple that you can teach this to a kindergartener[#THE]. First though, U have to teach Urself a basic fact of life that is, everything we Need and/or Use around us, costs us some resources in return. In simple terms, **there is a cost to everything we have in life**. In advanced countries, V take a lot of things for granted, like the air V breathe or the water V get when V open the tap. Around the time of this writing, for every 1 in 4 people globally, clean potable water is still a distant dream[#6]. In the 21st century we live in a society where almost anything is possible, just getting the basics is still an elusive task for a Third of the World Population, and it is a sad and scary truth.

Some might say that the **most important things in life are free**, like the air we breathe or the water we drink or the light we get from the sun. While it might be true for U, it **might not be true for another person** on the other side of this planet. If U live in a rural area then U enjoy nice fresh clean air, which might be scarce if U come from a bustling city. Potable water may be as easy as opening the kitchen faucet for some of U, while it may be an ordeal for someone from the dry inland areas of the world. While some of U might argue that money is not as important as any of those things, when U need money to get that fresh water or Oxygen, U will change Ur perspective about money. When U need money, U REALLY do need it for whatever purpose that it is for, it may not be as fundamental as Oxygen or Water, but I would say it is pretty close to it.

Some money management experts advise people to take a clear view of their financial picture by focusing on :

1. Earned Income
2. Passive Income Investments
3. Savings for Planned Expenses
4. Lifestyle Modifications

Just as any passenger car must have 4 tires, and each is equally important too, there are 4 elements to a sound financial plan. As the names suggest, Ur **Earned Income**, is the money U earn from Working. **Passive Income** is what U earn from Ur Investments, WITHOUT Working. **Savings** R what U shud be putting aside for future needs and for contingencies or unforeseen events in life, things U don't necessarily plan for. Crucially, **Lifestyle Modifications** are what makes Ur financial picture, Ur personal one. This is totally based on Ur definition of Success and Ur definition of

Happiness. (See Chapter 4). I give a lot of importance to Lifestyle Modifications Bcos oftentimes, U get in the rat race to prove that U R bigger and better than others but end up with debt and heartaches instead.

In the definition of a **Happy lifestyle**, no numbers R involved, millions and billions have no meaning except for the meaning U give them. U might be happy with a few 1,000s, while someone with millions may NOT be as happy when U look at them closely. U can choose a life to Show that U R wealthy, or U can choose to live a life where Only U know U R wealthy and U Don't have the need to prove it to others. What U do with what U have determines Ur level of success and happiness and ultimately Ur level of satisfaction.

In Ur younger years and through Ur teens, U R trying to understand everything around U and trying to fit in. When U R in Ur 20s and 30s, most of U will **worry about** what others think of U. In Ur 40s and 50s, U will come to a level of confidence and live like U **don't care** what others think of U. By the time U R in Ur 60s and 70s, U will discover that **others haven't been thinking about U** at all. (See Chapter 1). Whatever U do in life, do it to contribute to Ur Success and Happiness and not to prove something to others around U.

Some say borrowing money is not cool. Change that attitude to saying Borrowing money is good – if the borrowing is for the **right purposes**. Borrowing money (on credit cards, bank loans etc.) to buy useless fancy things to make U look wealthy is pointless. Instead, if U use the borrowed money for long-term investments or value addition to U or Ur personal space, then that is a smart strategy. What U do with that borrowed money is going to determine whether it was a good decision or bad.

Some say, "Buying that ___ made me happy," but after a while U realize that the happiness was probably just instant gratification and not something that gave U a sense of prolonged happiness. Everyone needs to indulge themself a little bit from time to time to satisfy that inner child. If U don't satisfy that part of Ur mind, it will sabotage the logical side of Ur brain and knowingly or unknowingly lead U to make the wrong choices and bad decisions later on in Life. As long as U have all the elements of Ur financial picture in good order, go for it.

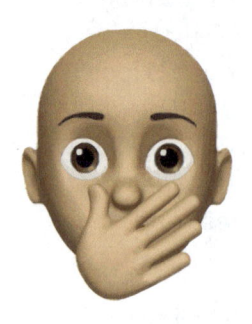

Whether U agree or not, everyone is playing the money game, and everyone wants to **win** the money game. **Winning** the money game boils down to being able to do **what** U want to do, **when** U want it and having that Choice. The **choice** of going to work Bcos **U want to** go not Bcos U have to go. When U have reached that point in life U can say U are beginning to win the money game. Whether U like it or not, U R playing the money game all the time. The only difference is, some play the money game to **win** and others play the money game **not to lose**. That simple difference in **attitude** differentiates people in the society.

When U play the money game to **WIN**, U go to earn a living – to make enough to support Ur desired lifestyle and make future plans so that some day in the future, U don't have to go to "earn a living" and can still enjoy Ur chosen lifestyle.

When U play the money game **NOT to Lose**, U go to earn a living – to make enough to support Ur current lifestyle and "hope that somehow" U will always have enough to support Ur lifestyle. There is No planning for the future in this way of Life, and U wonder why some people have to work way into their senior years of life. All it is – is a lack of planning and some poor choices along the way.

So how U play the money game will determine how Ur life story ends. And there is No Magic to winning the money game; all it takes is good money management skills. The 🔑 is skills. That means it is ***learnable***.

Once U learn it, make it repeatable and thus make it a **Habit**. The sooner U develop good money management habits the faster U can achieve what I call financial freedom – the choice of doing what U want to do, when U want to do it – without depending on anyone. Find the fun in it – It is a fun and definitely a fruitful habit to develop.

The same applies to the concept of **Time**. Lack of Time is never ever a problem, Lack of setting priorities is the actual problem. Setting priorities is another way of planning. When U don't plan ahead, U will be moving around aimlessly. Moving around aimlessly is like playing basketball without a hoop, U will be dribbling Ur time and passing around Ur responsibilities without scoring any results. The famous philosopher Plato said a few things that make a lot of sense like, Education should teach children to desire the right things in life, and the greatest wealth is to live content with little. Very profound statements if U think about them.

Don't be in the rat race to accumulate more and bigger and better **stuff** – it is all stuff anyway, and U R gonna leave it all behind too. U Really do not need a Lot to live Happy and Content, that is if U define Ur Happiness independent of the material things U Own.

Price vs. Cost

It is critical to learn the **difference** between the **Price** and **Cost** of anything U buy. Learning the difference between these 2 concepts will help U **manage Ur money** in the long term in everyday scenarios. The Price of an item is the amount U pay upfront to get it, while the Cost of that item is the amount U have to keep spending to be able to use it. So if something appears too pricey but has a much lower cost to operate then it will be a better buy when compared to an item that is very inexpensive to buy, but costly to maintain. Here R a few scenarios that will make the difference clearer.

U R in the market to buy a dependable flashlight, choice A costs 10 bucks while the choice B costs 15. A needs 4 batteries, each costing 2 bucks, while B needs 2 batteries. A, being cheaper comes with no batteries, B, being more expensive, already comes with batteries. A, being cheaper, is made with substandard materials, while B is made with more premium materials. Both flashlights will do the job, but we know for sure which is going to last longer and which one is likely to be backed by the manufacturer for defects. This example does NOT suggest that Expensive Items are always better (**that is a SAD myth a lot of people live by**). The lesson here is sometimes paying a little more for a product will get U a lot more VALUE for Ur money. So the Price alone should not be a final deciding factor for Ur purchase. Look at the value U R receiving for Ur money.

Here is another scenario. Say U print a lot of stuff for Ur work or School and Every time U go to the print store U spend on average 75 bucks/ month. Now if U were to invest 500 bucks in a nice printer / copier and keep it at home to fulfill all Ur printing needs, U can see that after a few months of use Ur cost is already steady and recovered while Ur price seemed too high to begin with. After a few months of use, U realize, U R Not spending 75 bucks every month, U have an asset already paid for and ready for future use, and there is only a fraction of cost every time U need to use this resource. In this case, Ur price to cost comparison will look like :

Time Frame	Cost of Ownership of Printer	Price U Pay for Printing Outside
Month - 1	500	75
Month - 2	0	75
Month - 3	0	75
Month - 4	0	75
Month - 5	0	75
Month - 6	0	75
Month - 7	50 (refill)	75
Month - 8	0	75
Month - 9	0	80 (Prices may go up)
Month - 10	0	80
Month - 11	0	80
Month - 12	0	80
Total at End of year	550	920
Average / Month	45.8	76.6
End of 1st year	**You Have an Asset for Future Use**	**You have nothing to show for**

What U do with What U Have???

As U can see the COST of buying a printer / copier was much higher than the cost of using the print store. But if U consider the long-term cost of using the store, U can see that it is Not the PRICE U should be focusing on but the Cost over a period of time. When we consider buying anything, the COST of owning the item, which is spread through the lifetime of the product, is far more significant than the Price of the item – which is a 1 time affair. This logic is more important when U plan to use that product for a longer period of time too.

What U have to Contribute??

When it comes to giving to others, there are mainly 2 things U can give, **Ur money** and other physical stuff or **Ur time** and other non-physical stuff. Sometimes, U want to give money and other things to some organizations of Ur liking, but U don't have the resources for it. Then give Ur time, volunteer for them. Sometimes U really cannot afford to spare time, but U want to support the organization, then give them Ur physical donations. Whatever U do, give or volunteer, do this out of the goodness of Ur heart, for other people. When U do, U will experience what is known as true **JOY**. U don't have to be rich or famous person to be a philanthropist: a simple act of kindness goes a long way in touching another living being's life.

Knowing the value of what U have

Some of U may have heard this story about a farmer, his son and the 20 year old car, others may have not, either way read it, U might like this version better:

There was this farmer whose son had just graduated high school with high honors and was getting ready to leave home for higher education. The farmer hands his son an old key and said, "Here, son. Take this key and go to the barn on the far end of the farm, and towards the back of it, under a tarp, is a surprise for you."

The son happily ran to the barn to find the machinery under the tarp and to his surprise he found an OLD car. OLD, really, really OLD. He was a bit disappointed but since it was a gift from his father, he went back to him and asked if it was ok to sell the car and use the money to get whatever he liked. The father said, "Of course U can son. It is Urs – so by all means do whatever U want to do with it. Just remember NOT to sell it to the first buyer U meet, make an effort and look one more step for a better buyer and confirm with me before U agree to sell." The son agreed and took the car to find a suitable buyer.

Bcos it was a used car, the son did the most sensible thing he thought of doing – he went down to the used car dealership in town and got a price quoted for his car. They offered him a whole 1000 bucks. He remembered his father's advice and did not settle for the first deal, so he went on to the local repair shop who sells car parts. This time around he was offered a better deal. They said the body looked old and worn, but everything inside the car was in great working condition so they offered him a whole 5000 bucks. Now this got the son very confused.

He went back to the farmer and said, "Father, the used car dealership only **offered 1000 bucks** while the used car parts store owner offered me **Five times more** – a whole 5000 bucks. I am a little confused about what is going on here". The farmer carefully listened

What U do with What U Have???

to the boy and then said, "Instead of selling it right away, **can U wait till next month** when we have the antique cars show in town??" The son reluctantly said, "I guess it wud be nice to have the money right away, but it probably wudn't hurt to wait a month until the car show, especially bcos of the huge variation in the offered prices." The boy was confused and anxious about the whole situation.

Days passed, and the annual car show came to town. The boy cudn't wait for the show to open up. He washed and wiped his car clean and polished it up a bit to attract better offers. Then he rushed down to the show and showed his car around. He came across some collectors. The first set of collectors were from his town and they looked at the car and offered him a **whole 100,000 bucks** for his OLD car.

After he picked himself up from the ground, he remembered his father's advice and went on for **ONE more step** for a possibly better buyer. This time he heard a lot of noise from the other side of the field, and he went over there to find some avid collectors from the big city. They checked out his OLD car: they popped the hood, checked out the engine, inspected the interiors and the transmission, paying attention to all the details. They discussed among themselves, and after about 20 minutes the lead spokesperson called the boy to the side and asked him what his expectation was. Being the smart kid that he was, and having learned about **basic negotiation skills**, he did NOT say a number and instead told them, they were the experts so he was willing to listen to their estimation. Impressed by the young boy's maturity, they offered him a whole **half of a million bucks**. The boy almost fainted and said to the collector, "Wow !! Really?? And why would that be?"

The collector said, "Well, son, what U have in Ur possession is one of the original 1967 Shelby GT500 Super Snake, one of a kind. Even the later ones built to spec costs a quarter of a million. So **would you accept our offer**?" The son, delighted by what he heard, ran back to the farmer and told him the whole story. The farmer smiled and replied, **"Boy!! Aren't U glad U waited?"**

Here's a few points to note from the story:
- ★ Know Ur worth – Don't always take the 1st offer.
- ★ People value U based on Their knowledge and awareness.
- ★ Delayed gratification is almost always worth it.
- ★ Negotiation Basics – **Never** go first on an offer.
- ★ Don't sell Ur Skills or Service to someone who doesn't know its value.

For most of Ur Life, U will be busy accumulating wealth and stuff for Ur loved Ones and those around U, and as U approach Ur Senior years, U will very quickly come to realize that there R Only 2 ways to choose from when U **Exit** from this world. There R only 2 ways U can **handle** whatever U have accumulated all throughout Ur Life. Either U can **Give it** and Go, or U can **Leave it** and Go. There is No Option of Taking it With U when U Go. The Difference is simple. When U decide to Give it, U distribute all Ur belongings to those around U or to someone in greater need, and find satisfaction in being generous. Or U can try to hold on to everything U earned and accumulated and leave it behind in a meaningless pile. The Choice is Urs, because one way or the other no moving truck will be allowed behind Ur hearse.

What U do with What U Have???

Here's what I do with what I Have...

ProcrastiNation

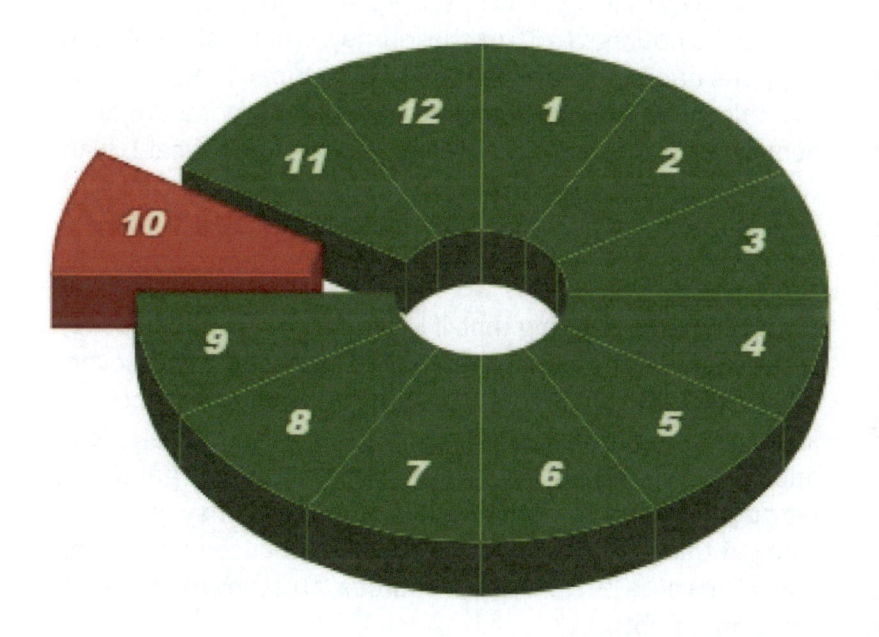

ProcrastiNation

☐ Now
☒ Later

I will tell you later on how this affects us all…

Of all the nations in the world that U know of, the most populous "nation" has always been ProcrastiNation, which is almost 2nd nature to most humans and the most **convenient habit** of all. V can all agree that ImagiNation is the most **powerful** of all, while ProcrastiNation is the most popular and most **destructive** of all.

Gotta love the saying, "The First Step in any journey is actually having the courage to **Start** the journey." That first step often happens once U have a clear mental picture of what U want to achieve: **Ur Vision**. Oftentimes U tend to procrastinate about taking action simply because U don't know what U want to achieve. This is not a bad thing as long as U eventually decide and then act. Once U define what it is that U want out of this Life, things become much easier (see Chapter 4).

Have U heard the saying that, if U ever want something **done**, U shud give it to a person who is **very busy** and have U ever wondered why that is?? Because they are the ones who know how to get things done through all sorts of obstacles and time constraints. Usually they are particularly good at **managing their time** and getting the job. The busy people who get things done are usually the more focused ones. They know the value of Time and resources, and they make the most out of both.

99% of the time, in most situations, a lack of time is **Never Ever** a problem. A **lack of Priorities** is usually the real underlying problem. As an example, U cannot NOT have time to have breakfast in the morning. If U feel U don't have enough time, U R'nt giving breakfast priority. That extra 5-10 minutes in bed is not worth it in the long run, and any health advisor will agree. Small acts of Procrastination like this can lead to long-lasting negative impacts in Ur life. So Choose wisely – think about the long-term effects of Ur actions.

Usually U can steer clear of Procrastination as long as U have Preset Goals and Visions for Ur future. Having Goals is sometimes as easy as having Dreams, but in order for a goal to be effective, it must create a change in lifestyle, attitudes and everything in between. The greatest labor-saving device invented in human history was Procrastination.

Most of U must have heard the following story about procrastination. There are several variations, one of which goes like this;

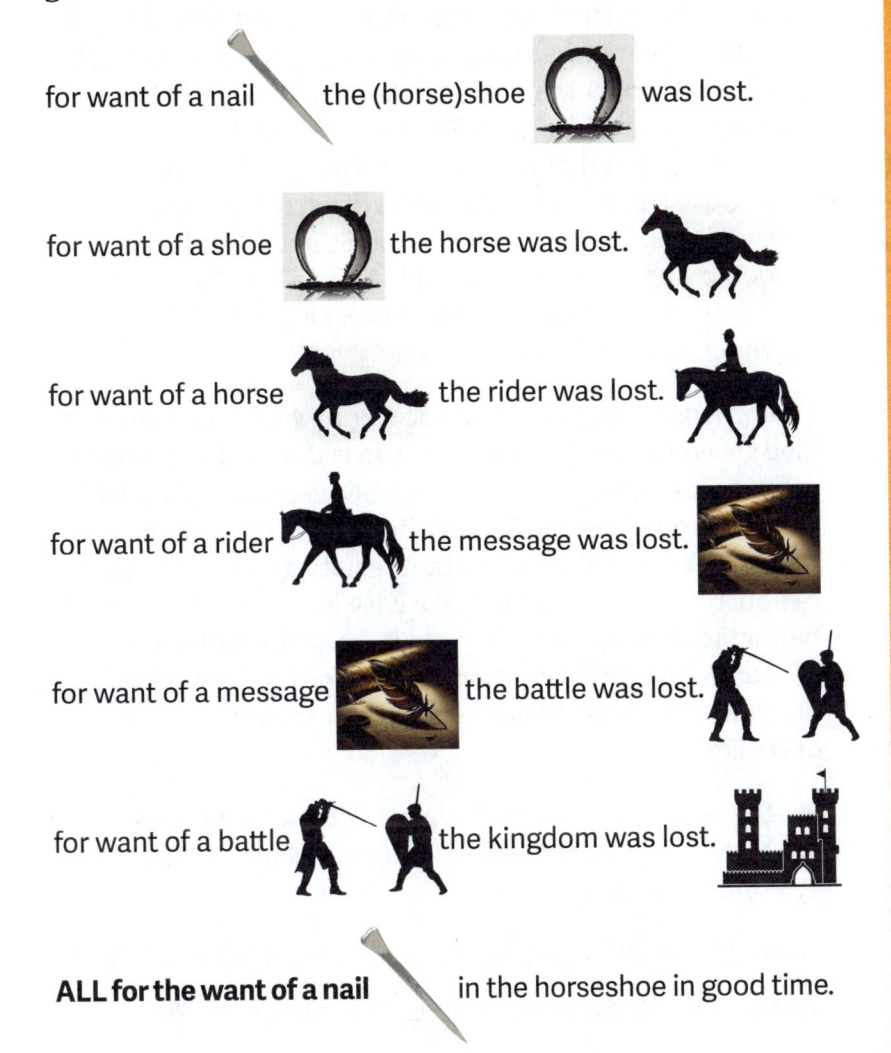

for want of a nail   the (horse)shoe   was lost.

for want of a shoe   the horse was lost.

for want of a horse   the rider was lost.

for want of a rider   the message was lost.

for want of a message   the battle was lost.

for want of a battle   the kingdom was lost.

ALL for the want of a nail   in the horseshoe in good time.

ProcrastiNation

In short, **don't put anything away for later**. Do whatever needs to be done When it is supposed to be done so that U see the results of Ur actions in a sensible timeframe. Whether it is a task that U hate to do, or a fun activity U Always wanted to try, do it and **Do It NOW !!** If you think Now is not the best time, you want to tell me a better time??

When U are in Ur 20s, U may be reluctant to act Bcos U R afraid of what **They** might think of U. Also Bcos one of Ur biggest joys comes from **Fitting In** to the cool group U R attracted to. By the time U reach Ur 40s, U wil decide to act as if U don't care what **They** think of U. By the time U reach Ur 60s, U discover that the so-called **They** have not been thinking of U at all, because **They** are living in their own world. So whatever it is that U SHUD be doing, go ahead and do it, because Nobody actually thinks of what U R doing. So when it is the time to study, Go And Study. When it is time to Work, Go And Work, and when it is time to Play, Go And Play like there's no tomorrow. Timing is very important. Don't put anything away for Later.

There's a famous saying by Wade Cook which has been modified several times, but the basic idea is that, If U Will do what most people won't do, for the next few years, then U CAN do – what most people Can't Do for the rest of Ur Life. Most people think short term – instant results and instant gratification. If U can work hard, make wise investments and make better life choices for the next few years (no matter what UR current situation is), then U can afford to have a happier, healthier and more fulfilling lifestyle for the rest of UR life.

For those of U who love to have fun with math, here's a fun activity and for those of U who hate Math, here's an Eye-opener for you.

Normal 100% effort + 1% more every day for 365 days $(1.01)^{365}$ = 37.78

Normal 100% – 1% less every day for 365 days $(0.99)^{365}$ = 0.025

360 Degrees of Life

Small changes can produce substantial results over a longer period of time. Everything takes its time, and as long as an effort is made in the right direction, it is all worth it. A small shift in Ur mindset is all that is asked for. Ur shift in mindset will affect Ur daily choices and Ur daily choices will affect Ur daily actions and that will ultimately affect Ur long-term results. Like Martha Beck once said, "***How you do ANYthing is how you do everything***." (emphasis mine) So if U R determined to improve Urself, just start by improving 1% at a time, small baby steps at a time towards Ur goals, instead of procrastinating. Then the results will speak for themselves.

Time management experts often point out that just as U have the **Habits of Doing** something, U also have the **Habits of NOT Doing** something. It could be as simple as NOT waking up 10 minutes earlier than required so U can have a peaceful breakfast for a fresh start of the day. That 10 extra minutes is usually courtesy of Ur friend called Procrastination, and that 10 Extra minute of immense attachment to Ur bedding will not provide any extra comfort for Ur body or mind. But if U use that 10 extra minutes of Ur day to peacefully wake up and go about Ur routines, that will make a big change. I am speaking **out of experience**, Try It !!! Totally worth it. Make a habit of waking 5-10 minutes earlier. If U normally wake up at 6:00 am, set Ur alarm clock for 5:50 am starting today. See the difference Urself.

Follow the simple 3-Rs for the new **Habit** formation:
- **Reminder** – the actual trigger that pushes U towards the new habit.
- **Routine** – inserting the actual NEW desired action into UR normal routine.
- **Reward** – the benefits U start seeing from this new habit, which may not always be instant.

It is a well-known fact that a Good Decision can become a Wrong One if the **Timing** is Wrong. There are plenty of proverbs from different cultures and times that support that statement. Few of the more commonly heard ones include:

★ A stitch in time, Saves Nine.
★ Make hay while the Sun shines.
★ Strike while the Iron is hot, etc.

All these proverbs pass on the same message : Do What is Needed to be Done, When It Shud be done, instead of **Procrastinating**. For example, U can have a nice branded car, but when the dash-light comes ON for Check-Engine, U better get the car checked up right away. It doesn't matter how expensive Ur car is or how clean U keep it, the car needs to get checked up, **U Do Not Procrastinate**.

Just like in the game of Chess, although every efficient player plays the game mentally at least 3 steps ahead of its opponent, they only make the Move when the time is Right for that move. This allows for U to change the moves as needed in response to the opponents moves, or whatever Life brings up.

No player can win the game by making moves ahead of its time, the same way in life we need to do whatever it is that we are **Supposed to Do** when we are Supposed to. In order to stay on course, **U Do Not Procrastinate**. U shud Plan Ahead, but Act when the time is Right.

When U have just had something hot and spicy, U really cannot procrastinate on drinking some fluids to calm down your tongue and taste buds. (Well U can; but

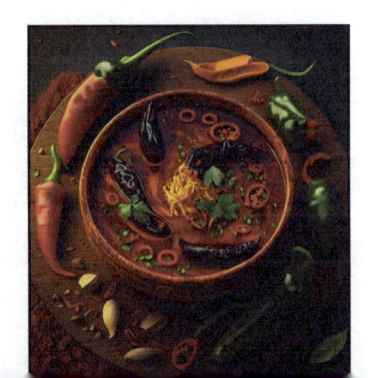

360 Degrees of Life

do U really want to??) Treat every scenario in life with the same urgency. Not because it will be the end of the world if U don't do it, but because U want to do the tasks U R supposed to do, to keep everything around U moving ahead. U will achieve Ur dreams and vision much more efficiently as long as **U Do Not Procrastinate**.

If U see a spark or ember at the wrong place, U don't need to wait till it becomes a full-blown blaze before U try to put it out. If that spark is appearing at a place where it is NOT expected, U wudn't wait around to see if it's actually growing into a bigger fire – **U Do Not Procrastinate**. U take control of the situation while it is still manageable. In the same way, perform Ur tasks when U shud.

When U procrastinate on taking action U run short on time and then U naturally become overwhelmed, that is IF U hold Urself **Accountable** for Ur actions. When U run short of time, U try to cut corners and take shortcuts and this is more dangerous than not doing the task itself. So when any situation demands Ur attention **Deal with It then** and there, Do Not put it away for later – **Do Not Procrastinate**. When U take actions in a hurry, the chances of making mistakes usually increase too.

A discussion of ProcrastiNation is never complete without a look at Time-Management. **Time** is One of the most crucial and nonrenewable resources at our disposal. As of this book's writing, there is No such Thing as Reversing Time. Once Time has passed, it falls into Past-Tense, meaning it is Done. **Time** – U Really don't know how much of it U have left in the **rest of Ur Life**. That is exactly the reason why it Really is a Smart Choice to Do it (whatever it is) **NOW!!!** Embrace the **Power of Now**.

ProcrastiNation

The only thing that is Real is whatever is Happening **NOW**, everything else is either a Memory from the past, or an Imagination of the future. What is happening NOW is all that U can see and feel and control. What has already happened is water under the bridge. It is done and gone, and it's now just a memory. What is going to Happen is all in Ur Imagination; what might happen depends on Ur planning and the steps U take towards it. There are numerous uncertainties along the way too, so always embrace the power of **NOW!!**

The Art of **Prioritizing** is a very desirable skill to develop all throughout Ur life. When U are in Ur youth, U need to prioritize the tasks that will help U move ahead in life towards Ur dreams and ambitions. When U become an adult, U should be prioritizing tasks that support Ur career advancements and family life. The fact of the matter is U R already managing Ur Time. The real question is – How?? The answer to this How determines the course of Ur Life.

How?

Several studies have proven that humans are **NOT** good with multi-tasking[#9]. So Avoid MultiTasking and **Eliminate Distractions** as much as possible. Ur cognitive capacity is reduced by simple distractions. Any level of innovative thinking demands extended periods of concentration, and every distraction will lower Ur productivity Bcos Ur brain needs time to **ReFocus** after each distraction. Once U prioritize Ur tasks, U have formed a system for attaining Ur Goals. Once U have formed a systematic approach for Ur actions, the only thing stopping U from reaching Ur Goals is Ur action steps.

Try NOT to approach a giant goal in one go. Instead, create several smaller steps towards the ultimate big goal.

360 Degrees of Life

This will eliminate the possibility of U procrastinating. When the goal U set is too far fetched, it is natural for Ur brain to say, "That's too far out to reach," and U will unknowingly feel overwhelmed and put it aside or put lesser effort towards it, thinking that all that is going to go waste. Instead, take the approach of creating smaller goals towards achieving the big goal and tackle each of them one step at a time. Break down Ur main task into smaller achievable steps and keep that as Ur progress checklist. Now as U complete each step, mark it off ✔. This will give U a sense of accomplishment along the way, and that can be Ur driving force towards attaining Ur ultimate goal.

Here's a list of a few things people tend to prioritize in life:

- ★ Health and Fitness
- ★ Wealth Management
- ★ Family Time
- ★ Personal Development
- ★ Career
- ★ Social Activities/ Service to Others
- ★ Hobbies/ Recreation
- ★ Mistakes / Negative stuff

How U Prioritize these things is Ur Choice, How U prioritize these also determine where U will put Ur Focus and Energy, Ultimately where U put Ur focus and energy becomes part of Ur Reality and Existence. So, Make sure to keep the main things – MAIN.

Time, as U know, is a Limited Resource – something that U can never ReCreate. So spend it very carefully. It is not going to wait for anyone either, so U gotta go with the flow and make the most out of Ur time. Whatever it is that Ur putting aside, U R taking away the most valuable resource from it – the time that it demands. Whether it is a task at work, a chore at home or a relationship that demands time, when it needs the time, prioritize it and Give it the Time it needs.

ProcrastiNation

Making the Most use of Ur time is a **Learnable Skill**. The busiest people in the world are the BEST Time Managers there are. They know the value of time, and they know that nobody gets an extra minute in the day. Everyone starts and ends with the same 24 Hours cycle, and they know how to make every minute matter. Become an EXPERT in Time management. Don't put aside anything for later (unless it is not a priority task) and see for Urself how Ur life will be Altered for good. There R numerous depictions of the idea of time management out there, and here is a simple one explained below, whether U have heard about it or not, it won't hurt U to read this version of the concept. Get Urself the following items and try it out for Urself, to understand this simple yet powerful concept of **Time management**.

1. A Jar with a wide opening on the top as shown in the picture with check mark
2. 3 Tennis Balls
3. 3 Golf Balls
4. 10 Glass or Plastic Marbles
5. 10 small nuts and bolts
6. Some Sand
7. A Bottle of water
8. Few Drops of Ur favorite color of paint

Assume the Jar U have represents the Amount of time in Ur Day. The Jar suggested has a very wide open mouth on the top to suggest that U have to be very broad and open minded as U start Ur day, Bcos U may face tasks of different nature and different sizes.

★ The Tennis Balls represent tasks and events of Life-Altering Nature.
★ The Golf Balls represent critical tasks that U and Only U can do.
★ The Marbles represent all the small tasks that demand Ur time and are Necessary for a healthy mind.

360 Degrees of Life

★ Nuts and Bolt represents the mistakes U make and the unexpected stuff from the day.
★ The Sand represents all the trivial tasks that take up Ur time.
★ The Water represents all the Cool Fun activities U can spend Ur time on.
★ The Drops of Paint represent Ur attitude.
★ Add Paint in the water bottle and Shake it Up for Colored water.

If U choose to have a very narrow-minded approach, guess what happens?? U R limiting Ur abilities to handle tasks of any significance, pretty much leading a superficial lifestyle some might say. So if U live a very narrow-minded life, then U can only fill Ur day with tasks of trivial nature, almost useless ones.

Now think of a much more open-minded approach, U can fill Ur day with all sorts of tasks. How U fill the jar determines how good U R with Time Management. If U just fill it with Sand or Water then for sure it will initially appear that Ur Life is Full of Fun stuff, but R U really making good use of Ur time?? Probably not.

Try **Not** to Fill Ur Jar in random order. Use a systematic approach to filling the Jar to clearly see that Ur life will be in balance and U will get a lot more accomplished. Assuming U had a major event that day, (not applicable on a daily basis – hopefully), drop a Tennis ball to represent that. U will see U still have room for other things. Now U drop 2-3 Golf balls, representing critical tasks. They may be time with/ for family, career development stuff, activities to keep Urself healthy and so on.

U can notice there is still room for the **smaller marbles** to fall in between those bigger tasks (the tennis balls & golf balls). The marbles would be tasks such as Helping a friend in need or Doing a selfless service to a stranger or Volunteering for an Organization whose values are in line with Ur values. As anyone who has actually tried to manage their time can admit, there are always some loose **nuts and bolts** that fall in front of U during any given day. These are things that U Don't expect to happen but happen anyway. Anything from a Traffic Jam to a slip 'n' fall. These are things U don't plan to spend time on, but happen anyway, and U R forced to spend time on them.

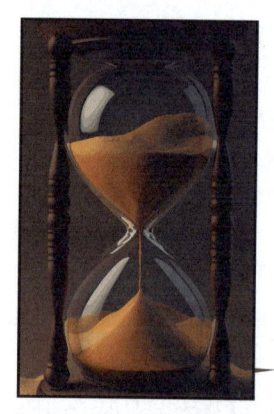

U will notice there is STILL more room for ALL those **Trivial tasks** that take up Ur time. They R like the **Sand** which is small yet occupies space or take up time from Ur day. These are normally Necessary activities like commuting, eating, laundry, grocery shopping just to name a few that wastes Ur time or takes up Ur time without actual positive contribution to Ur Happiness or Success.

Everything said and done, U can see that there is always room for some **water** in the mix. U can pour water (elements of fun) into Ur Jar (time in the day). And U will see how beautifully U can **Have Fun at Everything** U do during Ur Day if U have the right attitude. The colored water here represents Ur Attitude in Life. As U can see, if U have the right Attitude around EVERYTHING U do during Ur day, U will have a pretty positive outlook overall, and U will learn to find

360 Degrees of Life

the fun in every task U Choose to do. It is very critical that U don't fill Ur day first with the Sand (trivial tasks) because U will notice that U can fill up Ur entire day with worthless stuff, and, if U do, U will be very dissatisfied at the end of the day. Suddenly U will feel overwhelmed as to what happened to Ur day. U spent it on all these Trivial tasks, and now U don't have time for the useful tasks. It is same with just water – Having Fun should be more of an Attitude rather than a task in itself. U need to learn to Enjoy whatever U do, whether it is Ur work or doing a chore or helping Ur neighbor. Whatever it is, Do it with an attitude of Enjoying the task. Then before U know the task will start to seem easier, and U will start seeing that Ur performance will be improved and the results will be satisfying too.

Just like the great French revolutionary general, Napoleon had said, whatever U passionately and constantly desire, U always find a way to get to it. The only thing is U gotta set Ur mind on the right things and once U set Ur mind then don't fall back, go for that passion or dream U R pursuing, no matter what it takes or how long it takes, keep moving towards Ur goals and vision with vigor. The Thing to remember in this Journey is that, there is **NO ROOM** for Procrastination.

Ralph Waldo Emerson made a powerful statement about linking Ur Thoughts to Ur Destiny. He said something like, Ur Thoughts lead to Ur Actions, Ur Actions develop Ur Habits, Ur Habits carve out Ur Character and Ur Character will ultimately define Ur Destiny. Ur future, as U want it to be, is completely defined by Ur Thoughts and Ur Actions. U may have the most brilliant Thoughts, but if U procrastinate on Ur Actions, Ur Destiny will turn into just a Dream. Destiny is Never a Matter of Chance – It is Always a Matter of Choice. Choose Ur Actions wisely.

ProcrastiNation

I know I procrastinate on these...

Be Nice...

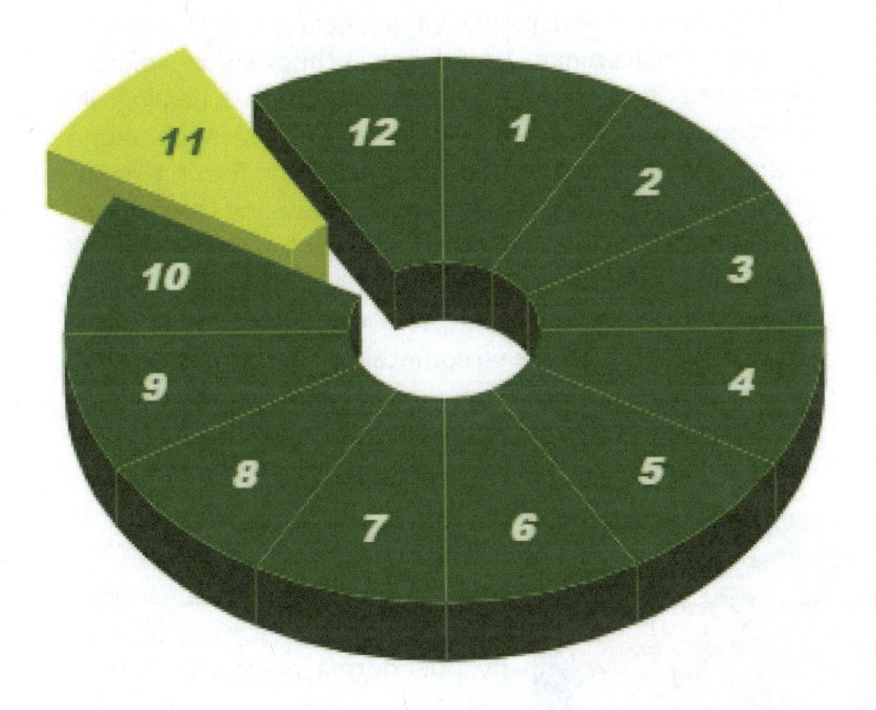

Be Nice ...
Try it, it almost always helps.

Be Nice in every transaction U undertake, whether it is with a friend, a relative, a mere acquaintance or Even a stranger. "Stranger Danger" is too old school, too passé and valid until U are in elementary school – maybe. Use Ur due diligence when dealing with strangers, but that doesn't mean U shud look at them with suspicion like some criminal or fugitive. Just Be Nice when dealing with everyone. Being Nice can be doing something for someone without any expectations of a returned favor. To some people it is almost impossible to behave that way, and they often have difficulty maintaining relationships too. Remember all human interactions do NOT have to be Trade based, in which something has to be exchanged every single time. **It is OK** to just Give or just Receive something from someone. That does not make U a person or greater or lesser value. It is all in the way U view Urself and the way U view Ur dealings with other humans.

Smile

Smile often and Smile Genuinely. It keeps you energetic and likable by most normal beings. Smile to tell others U R Human, Smile to let others know that U R approachable. Smile to let them know that U Care. Smile to tell Urself that U R willing to rise above Ur problems. There are a lot of messages U can pass along with a simple Smile. Use the power of the **Smile**. It is Free, and it is totally worth using. What Ur face muscles can do is beyond just vanity. It can actually bring forth joy and hope to others. Yes, just by the way U flex those muscles on Ur face. Don't believe it, Try It !! Like William A. Ward says, "A warm Smile is the Universal language of kindness."

Give 'n' Take

Being **Nice** can be a foundation to building **winning relationships**; relationships in which U give and not just receive. U must have heard that *it is better to give than to receive*. That is **NOT True**. For someone To Give, there has to be someone To Receive, and the same thing is true the other way around: for someone to Receive something, someone must be Giving it. So in a situation that is clearly 50-50, how is one better than the other?? In a healthy and balanced interaction between 2 or more people, there R always a lot of meaningful exchanges of values, be it physical or emotional. In no circumstance can we assume that one is better than the other, though it is true that it is better to be in a Position of Giving than to be in a Position of Just Receiving.

A nice poem I came across once read something like this:

Be **Strong**, when you feel weak;
Be **Brave**, when you feel scared;
Be **Humble**, when you are victorious;
Be **Nice**, **Everyday**.

Being Nice to someone actually is helpful to U as well. When U do something Nice for someone, Ur body releases an abundance of a chemical called Oxytocin, which gives U that warm and nice happy feeling. It puts U in a whole different state of mind.

Doing selfless acts are often considered Nice by others. Be Nice for the right reasons, don't fake it. Be Nice with the belief that Ur Nice gesture will encourage the receiver to Be Nice to others. Who knows, someday we might all decide to be Nice to one another, and this world of ours will be a much more peaceful place.

Be Nice...

Being **NICE** can be adopted as a LifeStyle, or it can be an Attitude. When someone describes U, can they confidently say that U R a Nice Person?? It is not easy to get that recognition, especially if U R fishing for it. People can spot a Fake person from a distance, so **be Genuine**, **be Truthful** in Ur Actions and Intentions. If U want to be Actually Nice and not just Appear to be Nice, it really does not matter what opinions others have of U, except when it comes to Ur personal progress and reputation. If people perceive U as a rude or selfish person, the chances of U becoming successful in anything U do will be very bleak. People generally tend to avoid those who are not Nice to them whether they R seeking help or Commanding support. People prefer to deal with others who are Nice.

Nice Gestures

You can be nice by very simple gestures like –

★ Holding a Door Open for someone,
★ Yielding for a pedestrian or another vehicle on road,
★ Saying a simple heartfelt Thank You,
★ Helping an Elderly person,
★ Helping a Disabled person,
★ Helping a Child,
★ Being a listening Ear to someone who is lonely,
★ Giving a shoulder to someone to Lean on,
★ Being the moral support for someone who is fighting a battle U know nothing about,
★ Just being appreciative of other people,
★ And so on the list can go on...

Be Nice to Everyone U have to deal with. Don't live with the fear that all strangers can be dangerous. If U do, U will have to live in a cave with Ur friends and relatives only, and V all know how that can end up. Be Nice to Ur Cashier at the Grocery Store, Be Nice to Ur server at the Restaurant, Be Nice to Ur custodian, Be Nice to Ur Mail carrier, Be Nice to Ur coach, Be Nice to Ur neighbor, Be Nice to Ur barista, Be Nice to Ur Boss (as much as U dislike them), Be Nice to Ur Co-Workers, Be Nice to Ur employees, Be Nice to Ur Kids, Be Nice to Ur parents. Be Nice to a Total Stranger – who knows, maybe Ur Nice gesture may be the only ray of sunshine in their life that day.

Forgive 'n' Forget

Mistakes leads to Anger, and Anger often leads to Hatred. This is True especially when the Mistake was made by someone else. If the mistakes were made by Urself, U tend to blame the situations and circumstances that led U to the mistakes and U forgive Urself for the mistakes and conveniently forget them too. Try to have the same attitude when dealing with others and their mistakes. Like Alexander Pope observed, It is human to err and divine to forgive. So as hard as it sounds, **forgive and forget**.

The moment U decide to Change Ur attitude towards other people's mistakes and treat them like U would treat Ur own mistakes, U know U have taken the first steps in attaining **Peace of Mind** and Spirituality. It will definitely be a New way to approach Ur Life – and it will be worth it in the long run. When it comes to having a Happy and Healthy life, one of the key ingredients to look for is **Peace of Mind**.

Courtesy 'n' Care

Sometimes showing Courtesy is an act of Kindness. Be Courteous in all Ur interactions, and U will start seeing that people behave in a similar way to U. Simple acts of Kindness can have long-lasting effects on others. Not only shud U **show** that U care through Ur words and actions but also U shud **genuinely care for others**. Several studies have shown that a vast number of people go to bed every night feeling unappreciated. They feel that no one cares for them. These feelings can lead to severe health issues in the long run. By developing an attitude of gratitude and kindness in Ur everyday interactions, U can spread good feelings and who knows someday more and more people may start modeling Ur NICE behavior. In the world of Scouting it is taught to ALL ages to Do a Good Turn Daily. **Baden-Powell**, the man who started the world-wide **Scout Movement** for Boys in England, said, "The real way to get happiness is by giving it to other people." He also said, "Try and leave this world a little better than you found it, and when your turn comes to die you can die happy in feeling that at any rate you have not wasted your time but have done your best."

The Parents/ The Elderly

For those of U who are fortunate enough to still have their parents or loved ones around in their lives ... here's a request, Let them grow old with the same love and affection they let U grow older. Listen to them speak and tell those same old stories again and again. Remember how U wanted to hear the same stories when U were a kid. Let them Win sometimes, in a game or in an argument – just like they did when U were younger. Let them enjoy their old-timers friends – just as they let u enjoy with Ur goofy friends. U don't need to embarrass them by correcting them in front of others. Let them be wrong, it is **OK**. If they spill while they eat at a restaurant, that is **OK** too. It is not like U never embarrassed them by knocking a drink over when U were a child. They did not disown U for that, so there is no reason to sweat over their small mess ups either.

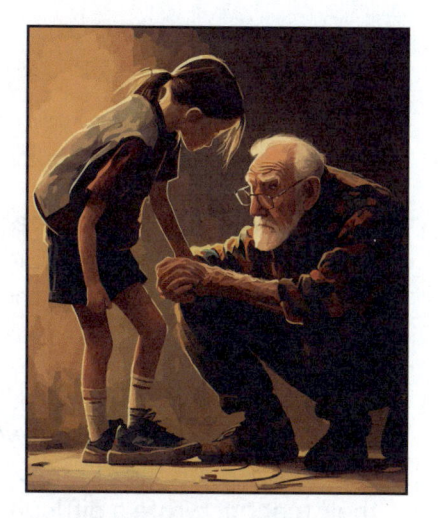

Don't take them away from their intimate surroundings just because it is inconvenient for U. They will feel like a plant that was uprooted and displaced from their natural habitat. They will wither and die. More often than not, they are not demanding much from U except Ur time. They will be understanding if U R not able to spare generous amounts of time because of Ur existing obligations and responsibilities. No matter how many material things U send their way, at their age none of those things have any value, and the only thing that will actually bring them Joy is the company of someone who actually Cares for them and gives them the feeling of Being Wanted and Being Loved.

Be Nice, and Let them LIVE the last stretch of the path they have left to go. Lend them Ur helping hand in their final years of life just as they lend their hand to U in the beginning years of Ur life. There's nothing more peaceful than to see Ur loved ones age graciously and comfortably despite all the physical ailments they may have.

Be Nice...

Loyal Friends

Here's the story of a boy who was tagged as stupid by his classmates:

I'm stupid

As a prank, a student stuck a paper on his classmate's back that said, "I'm stupid," and asked the rest of the class not to tell the boy. As any group of young kids would be, the group started to snicker and laugh on and off...

As the day went by, the boy wondered what was going on and laughed but didn't know Y. When math period came, their teacher wrote a difficult question on the board and challenged the class to solve it. The only one who dared to even try was this boy with the sticker on his back. He walked up to the board, wondering why everyone was still giggling, and carefully solved the problem. The teacher asked the class to applaud him and then removed the paper from his back.

The teacher then told him, "It seems that you didn't know about the paper your classmate had pasted on Ur back." The teacher then turned to the rest of the class and said, "Before I punish the whole class for the mischief and insult caused to this boy, let me give you *2 Life Lessons*:

1. Throughout Ur life people will put labels on U, some of them will be nasty and others will be intended to stop Ur progress." She went on, "Had Ur classmate known about the paper on his back, he probably wud not have gotten up to solve the question on the board." Silly labels like these that people put on each other usually inhibit people.

2. Teacher continued, "It is very clear that he does not have any loyal friends among you, Bcos nobody told him about the paper on his back." She said, "It doesn't matter how many friends U have – it is the loyalty U share with Ur friends that matters." It is not the Quantity/ Number of Ur friends but their Quality that actually counts.

360 Degrees of Life

U can learn a couple of valuable things from this simple story:

★ Ignore the labels people give U and Seize every Opportunity that comes Ur way to learn and grow.

★ If you don't have friends who will defend U behind Ur back, who can watch over U, protect U and Genuinely Care about U, then U R better off alone.

★ Have Loyal Friends and always have each other's backs.

Admire 'n' Praise

William A. Ward is renowned for his thought-provoking quotes and epigrams. Here's a Nice one to adapt, "Blessed is he who has learned –

★ to Admire but not envy,
★ to Follow but not imitate,
★ to Praise but not flatter, and
★ to Lead but not manipulate."

To wholeheartedly Admire someone for their accomplishments or characteristics requires a lot of confidence in Ur own character. It is easy to feel envious of others when U R only seeing the End results of the other person's journey. If U pay attention to the **Time** and **Effort** they put in to reach where they are in their Career or Life in general, then U will have more appreciation and Admiration for the person as a whole. This is why they say don't judge the book by its cover alone. Know the whole story before U pass a judgment, if U must.

When U **Praise** someone, let it be Genuine; let it not be some fake Flattery. When U praise someone, do it to highlight the best in them because, knowingly or unknowingly, this usually brings out the best in U too. In the same way, when U are

Leading someone, remember they are following U because they Trust U to lead them to better fulfill their vision too. Make sure NOT to manipulate those who are following U, as it wud be a breach of trust. When U Lead, do so with the pure intent for mutual benefit and progress. That is the mark of a Truthful Leader.

Toxic Behavior

U don't have to **belittle** someone or insult someone to make Urself look better. Lots of People are **Acutely Insecure** about their own abilities. The only way they feel comfortable is by belittling others around them. If U are constantly in the company of someone who behaves in that manner, then U will tend to act similarly. U too will develop a toxic behavior. The best thing to do is to Recognize the problem in Ur surrounding and Remove Urself from it Bcos it is jeopardizing Ur progress. Sometimes bad habits are formed because U R exposed to the wrong environment. And it is very true when they say that Environment can be stronger than will power – especially when it comes to Habit formation.

Once U recognize the problem and U get Urself out of that environment, cultivate positive Habits such as Being Nice to everyone, Respecting others and so forth. These Habits shud be so strong that they become a part of Ur character. Show Respect to people whether they deserve it or not. Not as a reflection of their character but as a reflection of Ur personality.

Not just Age or Mileage that Counts

Experience does not come just with age. U Gain Experience when U face different circumstances and handle them effectively. U can have numerous educational degrees or a high social status but if U don't know how to properly and politely talk to another human then Ur education has been a waste, and U R only as good as any ignorant person. A warm smile and a respectful demeanor is All it takes to break any language barrier across the world. Most humans understand that. (No need for U to go find exceptions to that – I'm sure there are some. Go with the words "most humans" – Focus on that.) Together, those two things can be summarized as Being Nice and Being Genuine. Doing this will go a long way to help U in most of Ur endeavors.

> It's Nice to B Important.
> It's way more Important to B Nice.

Be Nice...

I am a NICE person because...

360 Degrees of Life

Same Life - New Vibes...

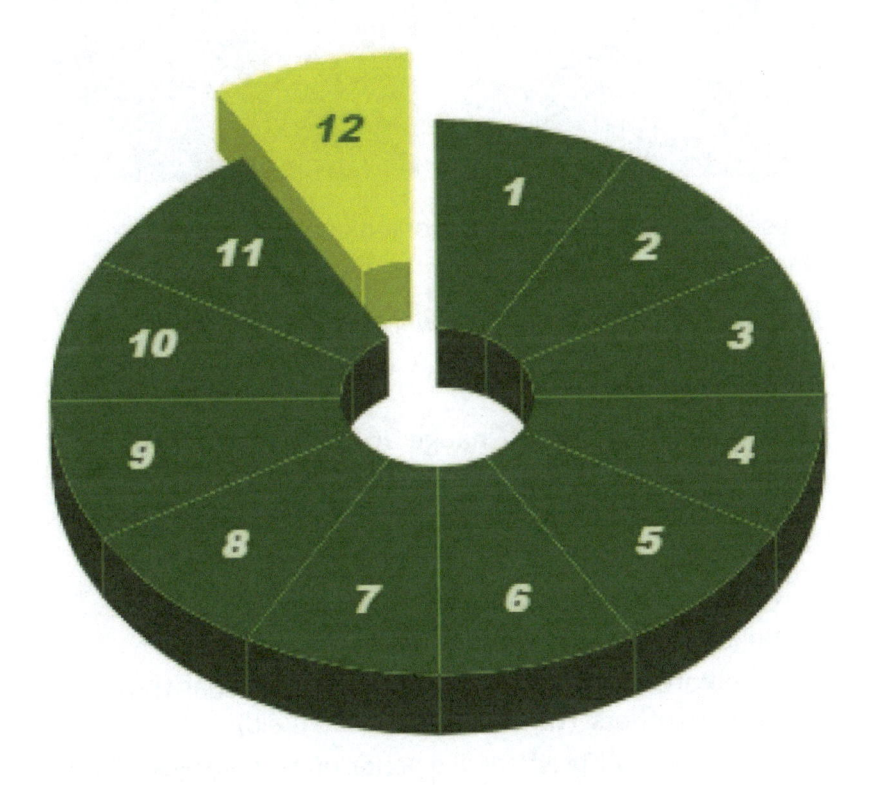

Same Life – New Vibes

These are just some new ways of looking at some of the things we all Already Know.

Read for fun and accept if you will or ignore if you want.

Some Nice Quotes:

- ★ 2 ways to be Happy – Change Ur situation or Change Ur mindset about it. (variation of Ben Franklin's)
- ★ After 2000 some years, Honesty is Still the Best Policy to adapt.
- ★ Always Dress for Success. (from John T. Molloy)
- ★ Build winning relationships in Ur Life.
- ★ Celebrate your Successes, no matter how small they seem to others. (variation of Jack Canfield)
- ★ Character and Trust are like paper, once destroyed, it's almost impossible to restore it. (variation of Oscar Auliq-Ice)
- ★ Every Master was once a disaster. (from T. Harv Eker)
- ★ Friendship based on business is much better than business based on friendship. (variation of John D. Rockefeller)
- ★ How you do Anything, is how you do Everything. (from Martha Beck)
- ★ If you can Dream it, you can achieve it. (variation from William Arthur Ward)

360 Degrees of Life

- ★ It is almost like a crime Not to have a Dream. (variation from Martin Luther King)
- ★ It's not what you say, but How you say it that matters.
- ★ Knowledge will give you power, but good character will give you respect. (from Bruce Lee)
- ★ Like the Scout slogan, Do a Good Deed Daily.
- ★ LIVE Ur life as if it is Ur last day, but PLAN ur life as if U R gonna live forever. (variation from Mahatma Gandhi)
- ★ Money can buy you Power, while Good Character can get you Respect.
- ★ Nobility is not a birthright, it is defined by one's actions. (variation from Ernest Hemingway)
- ★ Now is the only reality, all else is either memory or imagination. (variation from Osho)
- ★ The Best Way Out is Always Through It. (from Robert Frost)
- ★ The Last Teacher in Ur life will always be Ur Experience. (variation from Oscar Wilde)
- ★ Well Done is better than Well Said. (from Benjamin Franklin)
- ★ Whether you believe you CAN or you CAN'T; you are right. (variation from Henry Ford)
- ★ U Never Lose in Life, U either Win or U Learn. (variation from Nelson Mandela)

Some KOOOOOL ROOOOOLES:

- ★ Always be Grateful.
- ★ Add Value Everywhere you go.
- ★ Always request the late checkout.
- ★ Always Write down your Dreams.
- ★ Be Brave Enough to Admit a mistake.
- ★ Be confident and humble at the same time.
- ★ Be Nice to a Stranger.
- ★ Believe in Urself.
- ★ Change the world, don't let it change U. YOU are Unique.
- ★ Dare to Live the Life U have Dreamed for Urself.

Same Life – New Vibes...

- ★ Do everything with Passion, or don't do it at all.
- ★ Enjoy every little thing Life has to offer.
- ★ Give Credit to Others – Always.
- ★ Good Manners R what makes U a human.
- ★ If someone dares to admit a mistake, Forgive them.
- ★ If you don't go after what U want, U will never get it.
- ★ In a Negotiation, Never make the first offer.
- ★ Live in the Moment.
- ★ Be like a duck; be calm on the surface and paddle crazy underneath.
- ★ Make sure that Ur presence AND absence can be felt in someone's life.
- ★ Be Brave and talk to the most powerful person in the room.
- ★ Never shake hands sitting down.
- ★ Always Look the person in the eyes when shaking their hands.
- ★ Never turn down a breath mint.
- ★ Return a borrowed vehicle with a full-tank of fuel.
- ★ Stand up to Bullies and Protect those being bullied.
- ★ Take Pride in Everything you do.
- ★ Thank a Veteran.
- ★ Turn Ur Can'ts into CANs and Ur Dreams Into Plans.
- ★ U R only as good as Ur well-kept promises.
- ★ Unless U ask, the answer will always be NO.
- ★ Use Ur mind like a parachute, it works best when it's open.
- ★ When entrusted with a secret, keep it.
- ★ When U R angry, write it all into an email, read it carefully, then Delete it.

Some KOOOOOL and Powerful Words:

- ★ Accountability
- ★ Brave
- ★ Cheerful
- ★ Clean
- ★ Consistency
- ★ Courteous
- ★ Creativity
- ★ Dignity
- ★ Ethics
- ★ Friendly
- ★ Gratitude
- ★ Happy
- ★ Helpful
- ★ Humble
- ★ Integrity
- ★ Joyful
- ★ Kind
- ★ Love
- ★ Laughter
- ★ Loyalty
- ★ Manners
- ★ Morals
- ★ Neat
- ★ Nice
- ★ Obedient
- ★ Passionate
- ★ Patient
- ★ Quaint
- ★ Quality vs. Quantity
- ★ Respect
- ★ Reverend
- ★ Self-Confidence
- ★ Self-Respect
- ★ Thrifty
- ★ Trustworthy
- ★ Truthfulness
- ★ Upbeat
- ★ Vision
- ★ Valor
- ★ Worthy
- ★ Wholesome
- ★ Youthful
- ★ Zealous
- ★ Zesty

Same Life – New Vibes...

Same Life – New Vibes...

Different ways to split up the 360° of Life:

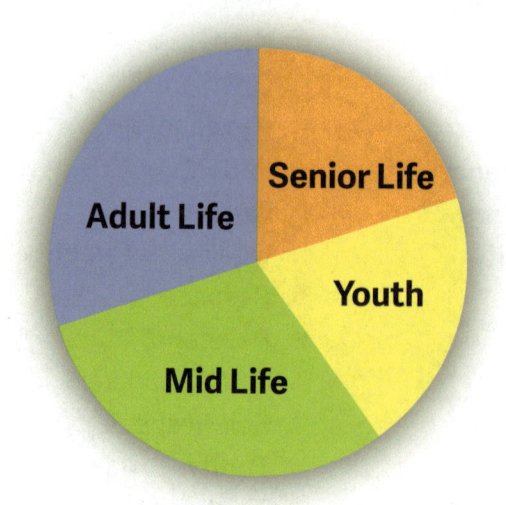

- Senior Life
- Youth
- Mid Life
- Adult Life

Measuring Yourself:

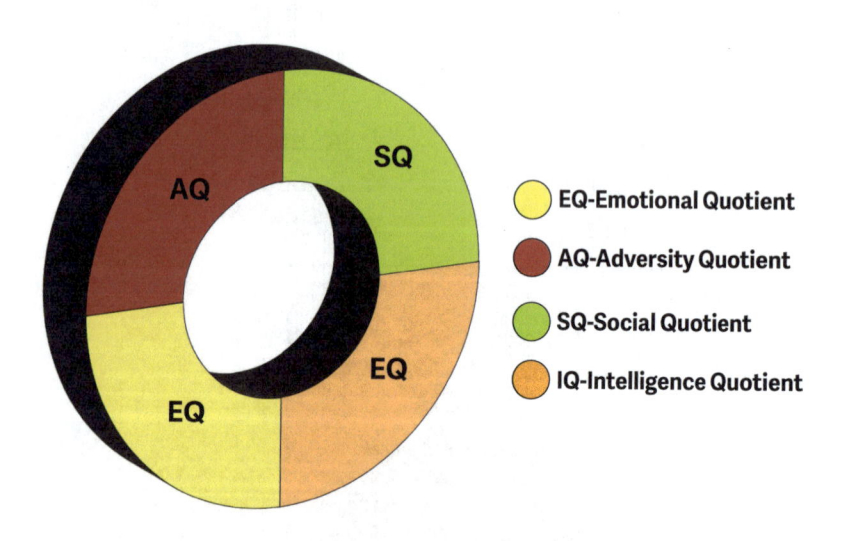

- SQ
- AQ
- EQ
- EQ

○ EQ-Emotional Quotient
● AQ-Adversity Quotient
● SQ-Social Quotient
● IQ-Intelligence Quotient

360 Degrees of Life

Ingredients to Successful Lifestyle:

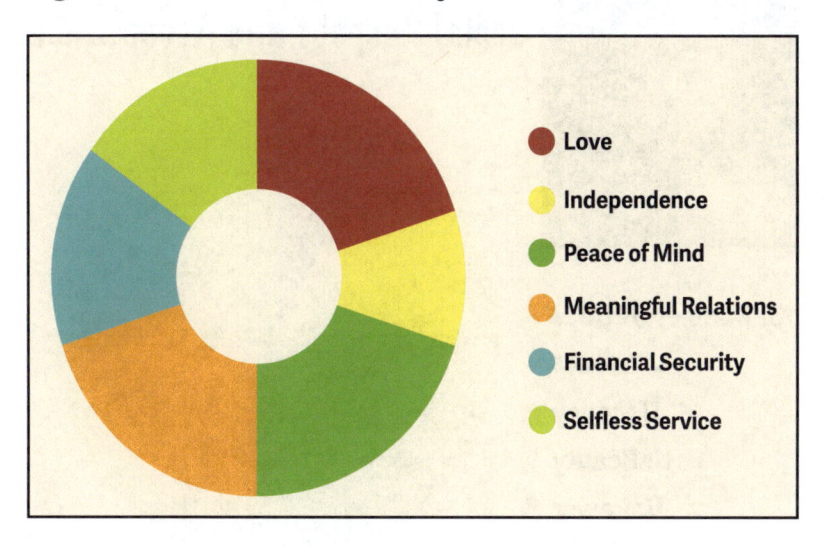

- Love
- Independence
- Peace of Mind
- Meaningful Relations
- Financial Security
- Selfless Service

Choose to be:

Friendly/Helpful
Trustworthy
Positive/Upbeat
Healthy
Kind/Courteous
Reverent
Obedient
Clean/Honorable
Loyal
Brave/Confident
Financial Savvy
Cheerful/Happy

Same Life – New Vibes...

175

Same Life – New Vibes...

Social Respect and Acceptance

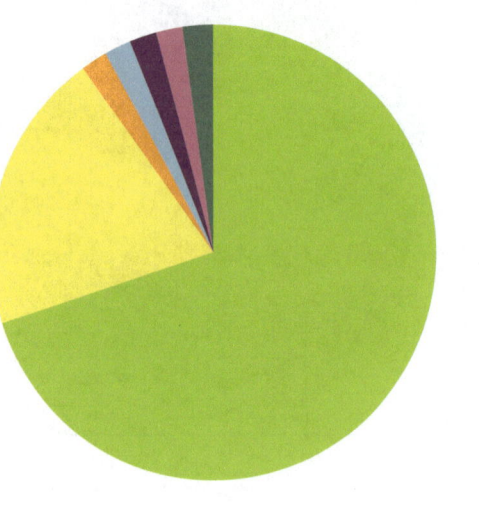

- Ur Manners/Ethics 🟢
- Ur Values 🟡
- U Money 🟠
- Ur Beauty 🔵
- Ur Power 🟣
- Ur Skills 🌸
- Ur Intelligence 🟢

**It's Nice to B Important.
It's way more Important to B Nice.**

360 Degrees of Life

References:

1. 4 Reasons Why Asking For Help Makes You A Stronger, Not Weaker, Leader by David Sturt and Todd Nordstrom Nov 1, 2017
2. theConversation.com, March 25, 2020; article by Isabelle Catherine Winder, Lecturer in Zoology, Bangor University, UK and Vivien Shaw Vivien Shaw, Lecturer in Anatomy, Bangor University, UK
3. "The Longevity Project: Surprising Discoveries for Health and Long Life from the Landmark Eight-Decade Study", Hudson Street Press, March 2011.
4. Livescience.com, Hard-working and Prudent? You'll Live Longer, Stephanie Pappas, March 15, 2011
5. Mind What You Wear: The Psychology of Fashion by Karen Pine
6. https://www.who.int/news-room/fact-sheets/detail/drinking-water
7. Contact Hypothesis, Developed in the 1950s by Gordon Allport, PhD and a variation of it from the University of California, Santa Cruz research psychologist Thomas Pettigrew, PhD and Linda Tropp, PhD.
8. Kipling, Rudyard (1910). Rewards and Fairies (First ed.). London: Macmillan.
9. https://fortune.com/2016/12/07/why-you-shouldnt-multitask/

Reference Abbreviations Used:

- BF - Ben Franklin
- EM - Elon Musk
- GBS - George Bernard Shaw
- HF - Henry Ford
- JJ - John Johnson
- MG - Mahatma Gandhi
- MLK - Martin Luther King
- MOT - Mother Teresa
- MT - Mark Twain
- NM - Nelson Mandela
- RWE - Ralph Waldo Emerson
- THE - T. Harv Eker
- WAW - William Arthur Ward
- ZZ - Zig Ziglar

About the Author

Native of New Delhi, India, Sreehari a.k.a. Hary, hung out as a teen way back when walkmans with cassette tapes were considered tech marvels, and Pac-Man, Tetris, Donkey Kong were the greatest video games ever built. The good ol' days when people used "Please" and "Thank you" generously. After gaining education as a computer engineer, and equipped with his unique and noted can-do attitude he emigrated to the United States at the turn of the century to further his studies and completed his Masters from the State University of New York.

After a few jobs in research, finance and service industries, he quickly uncovered his inner calling and stepped outside the comfort zones of a job and turned into a consultant and serial entrepreneur. Sreehari changed his name to Hary Nair, as a response to his adopted country's undying love for shorter names.

A careful venturing investor involved in tech, retail, and real estate, Hary is now settled in sunny Florida with his wife Vany and son Krish. As a teen Hary was an avid volunteer for HelpAge India, helping disadvantaged elderly. Today, his son's interests are aligned with his own, and together they are finding fulfillment in service and training to others through various roles in the Boy Scouts of America. When not busy with work or Scouts, Hary can be found behind the wheels, with a camera, on some country trails or at the course with his pitching wedge and 4 Iron.

For any questions, comments or commendations, Hary can be reached at: 360DegreesBook@gmail.com

Made in the USA
Columbia, SC
12 November 2024